Croatia

Discover Split, Dubrovnik, Plitvice Lakes and Adriatic Wonders

Embark on an Unforgettable Journey Through Croatia's Coastal Wonders and Cultural Treasures

By Robert Bryson

Copyright All rights reserved.

This book is protected by copyright. You cannot copy, store, or share any part of it in any format - electronic, mechanical, photocopying, recording, etc. - without prior written permission from the publisher.

The information in this book is for educational and informational purposes only. It is not a substitute for professional advice. The author and publisher are not responsible for how you use this information or any outcomes resulting from its use.

Every effort has been made to ensure the accuracy and usefulness of the information presented, but the author does not guarantee its accuracy or assume responsibility for how it is used.

Table of Contents

Chapter 1: Introduction **8**
    Where is the country of Croatia? 9
    Why should you visit Croatia? 10
    How Is the weather In Croatia 10

Chapter 2: Croatian Currency **12**
    How to Change Money in Croatia 12
    ATMs in the country of Croatia 12
    Credit Cards In croatia 12
    Camping grounds in Croatia 13
    Important things you should know about Croatia 13

Chapter 3: Planning Your Trip **14**
    The best times to visit Croatia 14
    Do you need a visa? 15
    What to Bring to Croatia 15
    What language do Croatian speak? 16
    Travel Insurance 16
    How much it costs to travel to Croatia 17

Chapter 4: Getting There and Around The Country **18**
    How to Get to Croatia: Airports and Transfers 18
    Public Transportation: You can take buses, trains, and ferries to get around. 18
    How to Rent a Car 19
    Chapter 5: Accommodation 20
    Hotels in Croatia 20
    Apartments in Croatia 21
    Villas In Croatia 21
    Campsites 21
    Which Accommodation Is the best for you? 21

Chapter 6: Top Attractions **24**
    1. Dubrovnik 25
    2. Diocletian's Palace in Split 27
    3. Plitvice Lakes National Park 28
    4. Hvar Island 29
    5. Korčula Island 30
    6. Rovinj 31
    7. Gornji Grad in Zagreb 32

8. Rijeka 33

9. Taking a boat tour of Kornati National Park 34

10. Mljet National Park 35

11. Trogir 36

12. Sibenik 37

Chapter 7: Outdoor Activities and Nature **38**

Hiking in Paklenica National Park 38

    The best way to get to Paklenica National Park from Zadar 38

    Take bus 38

    Drive 38

    Get a taxi 39

    How to Spend Your Time in Paklenica National Park 39

    Hiking in Paklenica National Park 39

    Visit some Caves 40

    Climbing 40

    Taking pictures of nature in Paklenica National Park 40

    Paklenica National Park Restaurants And Accommdations 41

    Exhibition of an Underground Bunker 41

    Ethno Houses 41

    When Is The Best Time To Hike In Paklenica National Park? 41

    How Long Can You Stay in the Park? 42

    Cost to get into Paklenica National Park 42

    Is it safe to hike in Paklenica National Park? 42

    What to Bring to Paklenica National Park for a Day Hike 43

Going Sailing Or Boating Along The Coast Of Dalmatia 44

    Why Sail in Croatia's Dalmatian Coast? 44

Seven Beautiful Places To Stop While Sailing Along The Dalmatian Coast 45

    1. Split 45

    2. Hvar 45

    3. Korčula 46

    4. Makarska 46

    5. Trstenik 47

    6. Dubrovnik 47

    7. Mljet Island 48

Chapter 8: Scuba diving **49**

Dive around the famous shipwrecks in Istria 50

Pula	51
Medulin	51
Rovinj and Porec	51
Snorkeling	51

Chapter 9: What to expect: why snorkeling in Croatia is a good idea 53

1. Clean water	53
2. Very good underwatervisibility	53
3. Diverse Marine Life	54
4. Shipwrecks, caves, cliffs, reefs, and corals all under the water	54
5. Safe Ways to Snorkel	55
6. Cheap and accessible	56
7. Warm Weather	56
8. Coast and islands that look beautiful	57
9. Experience the Culture	57

Chapter 10: These are the eight best places in Croatia to swim 58

1. The National ParkBrijuni	58
How to Get There	59
2. The Cape Kamenjak	59
How to Get to Cape Kamenjak	59
3. Hvar Island	60
How to Get There	60
4. Makarska Riviera	61
How to Get Around	61
5. Vis Island	62
How to Get There	62
6. Mljet Island	62
How to Get There	63
7. Dugi Otok	63
How to Get Here	64
8. Split	64
How to Get There	65

Chapter 11: Tips on How to Snorkel in Croatia 66

Pick the right time	66
Bring along your equipment	66
Go along with water shoes	66
Respect the environment	66
Be careful	66

Rafting and kayaking in the Zrmanja River 67

Chapter 12: Food and Drink 68
Croatia traditional foods 68
    Meat Dishes 68
    Seafood Dishes 69
    Croatian side dishes and salads 71
    Croatian restaurants dessertsand sweets 71
Regional dishes 72
    Food in Istria 72
    Truffles: The Istria's culinary gold 72
    Food in Dalmatia 73
    Foods in Zagreb 73
    Foods in Slavonia 74
    Food and drinks in Kvarner Gulf 74
    Food and drink in inland Croatia 74
    Pršut 75
Meals in Croatia 76
    Breakfast in Croatia 76
    Lunch in Croatia 76
    Snacks In Croatia 76
    Cooking your own food in Croatia 77
    Eating out in Croatia 77
    Croatian street food 78
    Vegetarian In Croatian 78
Drinking in Croatia 79
    Alchohol in Croatia 79

Chapter 13: Shopping In Croatia 82
Five best places to shop in Croatia 82
    1. Arena Centar 82
    2. Mall of Split 83
    3. The Portanova 83
    4. Shopping Center SRD 83
    5. SubCity Dubrovnik 84
Things to Buy When You Go Shopping in Croatia 84

Chapter 14: Nightlife and Entertainment 86
Top 15 Places to Have a Good Time at Night in Croatia 86
    1. Deep Makarska 86

 2. Pag Island's Noa Beach Club 87

 3. Boogaloo, Zagreb 87

 4. The Aquarius, Zagreb 87

 5. Alcatraz,Zagreb 88

 6. Banje Beach Restaurant and Nightclub in Dubrovnik. 88

 7. The Kiva Bar 88

 8. Carpe Diem 89

 9. Hula HulaBar and beach 89

 10. Akvinta Party Boat, Makarska 89

 11. The Academia Club Ghetto in Split 90

 12. The Club Crkva in Rijeka 90

 13. The Club Aurora and Primosten 90

 14. The Aquarius Club in Zagreb 90

 15. Zagreb Art Gallery 91

Chapter 15: In conclusion **92**

 1. Be focused 92

 2. Do not just visit Dubrovnik. 92

 3. Get the best beds by booking early 93

 4. Enjoy the island life 93

 5. Take a wild walk 94

 6. Learn their culture 94

 7. Eat very well 94

 8. Drink responsibly 95

 9. Learn some slang 95

 10. Your health matters 96

Chapter 1: Introduction

Are you excited to see Croatia for the first time but don't know what to do? If you want to visit Croatia, this is the complete guide you need.

You should go to Croatia! Croatia has beautiful beaches, historical sites, nature wonders, exciting activities, tasty food, and pretty coastal towns.

A lot of people who are going to Croatia for the first time are worried about how safe it is. They don't know where to go or how many days they need to stay in Croatia. Don't worry! This is a safe place for tourists to visit. There is almost no crime there.

You will be very safe in Croatia, even if you are a woman going alone.

This travel guide has tips for people who are going to Croatia for the first time. In this travel guide, I talk about some of the most common worries, myths, and general advice. I hope you can use these tips for your next trip to Croatia, even if you've been there before.

Where is the country of Croatia?

Let's clear up the basic facts first before going on. Croatia is a country in the Mediterranean Sea that connects the Balkan states to Central Europe.

It is on the Adriatic Sea, east of Italy and west of France. In the north, it shares borders with Hungary. In the southeast, it shares borders with Bosnia and Herzegovina. In the east, it shares borders with Serbia. in the south, it shares borders with Montenegro.

Why should you visit Croatia?

Croatia is a beautiful place on the Adriatic Sea that draws tourists with its mix of historical sites, natural beauty, and cultural diversity.

From Zagreb, the lively capital, in the north to Dubrovnik, a must-see destination with its unique mix of cultural heritage, beautiful beaches, and high-end resorts in the south, and all the way to PlitvičkaJezera's waterfalls, Slavonija's cultural wealth, and the islands' peace and quiet, Croatia offers a journey that goes beyond the ordinary.

Embrace the diversity, and let the different parts of Croatia make your trip unique.

How Is the weather In Croatia

There are three different temperatures in Croatia: a continental climate in the middle, a Mediterranean climate along the coast, and a mountain climate above 1200 m.

It usually rains less in the winter along the coast, but it can be dry, hot, and sunny in the summer.

The weather is usually warmer and sunnier in Dalmatia, which is in the south of the Adriatic Sea, than in Istria, which is in the north.

Temperatures can change by up to 5°C (40°F) every day.

The normal temperature in the summer is about 22°C (72°F), but in July and August, there are more than 40 days when the temperature is over 30°C (86°F).

Most days in the winter are around 10°C, and January is the coldest month, with daily averages of less than 10°C (50°F).

In the summer, the sea is 25°C (77°F) and in the winter, it is 12°C (54°F).

The climate in the middle part of Croatia is mild and continental. It's cold and foggy in the winter, and hot and dry in the summer.

The average temperature in the summer is 22°C (72°F), and the average temperature in the winter is 4°C (40°F).

Chapter 2: Croatian Currency

Since January 1, 2023, the Euro, a shared European currency, has been used as the currency of Croatia. At the time this piece was written, $1 was worth €,0.93, £1 was worth 1.19 €.

How to Change Money in Croatia

A "no commission policy" is advertised by most of the exchange offices. Even though they don't charge a fee, they decide the exchange rates on their own.

These prices can change a lot. Look out for these differences and compare prices to find the best deal.

ATMs in the country of Croatia

When you need to get cash out of an ATM, try to use one that is owned by a real bank. For example, Zagrebacka, Erste, Adikko Bank or Privredna OTP should have a sign on it.

Most of the time, these ATMs are near where the bank has branch offices.
You can often find Euronet (blue and yellow) or Auro Domus (yellow and black) ATMs in spas and hotels, as well as any other type of ATM that isn't a bank. The fact that they are usually put in more visible places in towns, hotels, and vacations makes them easier to use, but they cost more.

If, on the other hand, ease of use is more important to you than a few dollars here and there, there you go.

Credit Cards In croatia

In Croatia, credit cards are accepted in many places, but not all of them.

When you get to Croatia, one of the first things you'll notice is how many ATMs there are.

Some restaurants and bars, as well as smaller companies, would rather take cash. As a general rule, you should be able to pay with a credit card if you see a sticker near the cashier or on the door. But the only sure way to find out is to ask.

There is something else you need to know about money that is called "dynamic currency conversion." This means that the amount of your credit card transaction is changed to the currency you normally use at the place of sale, not by the company that issued your card.

When you use a credit card to pay in a hotel, restaurant, or other business, the staff will ask if you'd like the charge to be made in Euros or your own currency.
In theory, you might sometimes make money by being charged in your own currency by a seller right then and there, but in practice, this doesn't happen very often. You'll just pay more than you would have otherwise.

That's why you should always pay with the local money. You could also ask about the exchange rate and then compare it to the rate you see online that same day.

Camping grounds in Croatia

A lot of people also like to camp in Croatia. Lots of campsites are along the coast, but only a few are in the rest of Croatia.

Lanterna in Porec, Valkanela in Vrsar, Polari in Rovinj, Park Umag, and Zaton near Zadar are some of the most popular parks in Croatia.

Important things you should know about Croatia
- 3,986,627million people lived there in 2021.
- Zagreb is the capital;
- Split, Rijeka, and Osijek are the other important cities by population.
- The Latin writing is used for the language Croatian
- The Euro is the currency
- Has a Size of 56,691 square kilometers
- The main religion is Roman Catholic, and the main ethnic group is Croatian, which makes up almost 90% of the people.

Chapter 3: Planning Your Trip

The best times to visit Croatia

June and September are the best months to go to Croatia. The weather is still warm and sunny, prices are lower, and the sea is warm enough to swim in. There are also a lot fewer people around—there are no lines, traffic jams, or crowded beaches.

One more thing: the sea is warmer in September than it is in June.

Also, keep in mind that Croatia is very popular with Austrians and Germans, especially the Istria and Kvarner areas in the northern Adriatic. When German schools are out for the summer, like during Corpus Christi, which can be in mid-May to early June or late May to mid-June depending on the year, there are more people and places to stay cost more. This is true, but it also means that hotels often have deals for June when the German school breaks are in May. It goes both ways.

Do you need a visa?

Most people from other countries, like those from the EU, the UK, Canada , the USA, Australia, and New Zealand, don't need a visa to visit Croatia.

People from those countries can come to Croatia and stay for up to 90 days in a 180-day period.

Citizens from EU countries can enter Croatia with just their ID cards. Everyone else must have a legal passport.

If you need a visa to visit Croatia but already have a valid Schengen visa and visas for Romania, Bulgaria, Cyprus, and Croatia, you don't need a separate visa for Croatia. You can visit Croatia as long as you have a valid visa from one of the countries listed above.

What to Bring to Croatia

We all pack in our own unique ways and follow our own rules when it comes to packing for journeys.

Croatia has four seasons and three different temperatures. Along the coast, it has a Mediterranean climate, in the mountains it has a mountain climate, and in the middle of the country it has a continental climate.

This means that most of the clothes you bring to Croatia in the summer should be light.

 No matter what, a windbreaker jacket, long pants, and tights are always useful. For the rest, bring some shorts and tops that you can mix and match, or some easy summer dresses.

Remember to bring your water shoes and swimsuits and cover-ups, sunscreen, and a microfiber towel to the beach.

 You should also bring sandals, walking shoes, and a money bag for traveling.

Also, because of weight and size limits on bags, it's best to buy light luggage if you're going to Croatia.

Also, don't forget your camera gear (with lots of extra batteries), a waterproof phone case, plugs, converters, and any other small items that you will need in Croatia.

Plugs type C and F work with 220V and 50 Hz in Croatia. Both plugs look the same and have two round points that are 19 mm apart.

What language do Croatian speak?

A lot of Croatians know English as a second language, but German and Italian are also very popular, mostly because so many German and Italian tourists come to the country every year.
Most people who work in the tourism business and younger people speak English pretty well. This is especially true in Istria, along the coast to Dubrovnik, and in Zagreb, the capital.

Older people don't usually know English, but they might be able to talk to you in German or Italian. If you know Polish or Czech, you may find some words in Croatian that are related.

Some folks may also speak Russian or French. During the communist era, Russian was taught as a second language in schools, so many older people can speak it. However, English is now mostly spoken by younger people.

Croatian is hard to learn because it sounds a lot like Serbian and Bosnian. However, people who live there like it when tourists use it for simple things like saying hello and thank you.

Travel Insurance

If something goes wrong, travel insurance will cover a lot of different situations, such as lost bags, trip cancellation, and medical help.

With an EU medical insurance card, you can get basic medical care and care in an emergency if you live in the EU. But it doesn't cover getting back to your home country in an emergency.

People who are not from the EU should check with their embassies to see what kind of medical care they are covered for in Croatia. This is because it rests a lot on the agreement between the two countries.

You will definitely need to buy travel insurance in case of other damages, such as losing documents or bags, losing your belongings, or having to stop your trip. There are many companies that offer travel insurance with a range of coverage choices and packages.

How much it costs to travel to Croatia

Croatia is about the same price as the rest of Europe for a holiday. It's not as expensive as some high-end spots in Europe.

Each week, it costs about $718 (kn 5,049) for one person to travel in Croatia and about $1,436 (kn 10,097) for two people. This amount covers a place to stay, public transportation, and cheap things for sightseeing.

Flights from the UK can cost up to £300, or you can take a bus ride that takes 32 hours and costs between £30 and £85.

If you fly from the US, it will cost more. Say you want to go from New York John F. Kennedy International Airport to Zagreb Airport Franjo Tuđman. It takes 13 hours and costs about $1,814 to fly round-trip.

Chapter 4: Getting There and Around The Country

How to Get to Croatia: Airports and Transfers

It's easy to get to Croatia from anywhere in Europe. There are direct flights from many European cities to all of Croatia's big towns from April to September. Also, you can fly between Split and Zagreb and the rest of Europe all year long.

You can also take a bus from other European cities to get to Croatia. It can be hard to find bus plans because there are so many companies that run the service.

Public Transportation: You can take buses, trains, and ferries to get around.

A car is the best way to get around Croatia. It's worth taking a side trip to Croatia, which is a small country with great roads and cute little towns. Taking a car is the only way to really see the country.

The bus is another great way to get around Croatia. Buses are new, quick, cheap, and often available. I only don't think you should take the bus to the islands and Istria. Finally, if you have to travel but can't drive, take the bus and enjoy the ride.

Most people still take ferries to get to the islands, and sometimes they're the only way to get there. Rijeka, Zadar, and Split are the main boat ports, but ferries also leave from Brsecine, Makarska, Drvenik, Orebic, Ploce, and Prapratno, which are smaller coastal towns. The biggest ferry company in Croatia is Jadrolinija, and its boats go on most of the lines.

In bigger cities, public transportation works well and is effective. City buses run in Split, Rijeka, Zadar, Pula, and Dubrovnik. In Zagreb, there is a large network of electric trams and city buses. It takes about 2€ to ride the bus or train.

Aside from Zagreb and Rijeka, most taxi rides are expensive.

However, since Uber came out in 2015, taxi rides have become more cheap. Most well-known vacation spots, like Zagreb, Split, Rovinj, Dubrovnik, Zadar, and more, offer UberX.

Uber and Cammeo Taxi are the most affordable ways to get a taxi in Croatia. Both companies, though, change their prices based on demand, and prices usually go up during the busiest tourist season.

How to Rent a Car

A car is the best way to see all of Croatia. Also, don't be afraid to rent a car in Croatia if you don't have your own. You can stop wherever and whenever you want, see more in less time, and take in the sights.

Croatia's car hire business is only open during certain times of the year. This just means that if you want to go to Croatia in July or August, you'll need to book your hire car a long time in advance. In addition, this means that rental prices go up a lot during these two summer months. When you rent a car in Croatia, i suggest that you use Rentalcars.com.

Chapter 5: Accommodation

There are many places to stay in Croatia, such as hotels, hostels, flats, villa rentals, and campgrounds. Which one is best for you relies on how you like to travel and how much money you have.

The main idea behind Croatia is that it is a great place for families. Some places, though, are better than others. This is especially true for Hvar Town, Dubrovnik, and some parts of Rovinj.

There are six main types of places to stay in Croatia:

- Apartments
- Small, private inns
- Two- and three-star hotel resorts for regular tourists
- Five-star luxurious hotels
- Lighthouses
- Small or private islands

Hotels in Croatia

Zagreb, Dubrovnik, Rovinj, and Losinj Island all have a good selection of 5-star hotels. Some hotels in Croatia offer an all-inclusive plan, but all-inclusive vacations aren't very popular there.

When people talk about "all-inclusive" in Croatia, they usually mean a full board meal plan with unlimited drinks during meals. There are many hotels in Croatia that offer a half-board meal plan. If you buy dinner as part of your room rate, it's often a good deal.

Apartments in Croatia

A lot of Croatians rent out their homes to tourists. Instead of hotels, you could stay in an apartment. They cost less, have more room, and come with a kitchen that is fully stocked.

It's the same for apartment rentals as it is for hotels: they need to be licensed and get a star grade. The best places to find apartments to rent in Croatia are on Booking.com and Airbnb.

Villas In Croatia

Ville rentals are another popular and growing type of lodging. These villas are mostly away from the busy tourism areas, so they offer peace and quiet and a lot of privacy. Also, houses have pools where you can relax all day.

Campsites

Another great way to stay in Croatia is to go camping.

A lot of people like to camp in Croatia. Lots of campsites are along the coast, but only a few are in the rest of Croatia.

Lanterna in Porec, Valkanela in Vrsar, Polari in Rovinj, Park Umag, and Zaton near Zadar are some of the most popular parks in Croatia. This website, Camping.hr, is run by the Croatian Camping Association and is the best place to learn about camping in Croatia.

Which Accommodation Is the best for you?

You might already know the answer! It depends on how you like to travel and how much money you have.

It's easy to find a place to stay in Croatia. You can find all kinds of places to stay. You can easily find and book a place to stay in Croatia, as you will see.

But it might take a while to find the right place to stay for you.

Hostels can be great places to meet other tourists if you are going on a trip by yourself. Also, don't forget that most hostels in Croatia have private rooms with bathrooms right next to them, even if you don't like dorm-style rooms.

It's likely that you and your partner will want to look at both hotels and vacation homes. Some places are even just for adults.

When you go to Croatia with your family, many of the places have family rooms and a half-board plan. You can save a lot of money on food and time by doing this.

You don't want to stand in front of the stove all vacation.

You can, however, rent a large apartment or a mobile home on a park and cook your own meals if money is tight. You know that hotel food is fine for a few days, but after that, you'll want to eat something you made yourself.

How to Find and Book a Place to Stay in Croatia finding.com is by far the most popular site for finding places to stay in Croatia. There is only one website, Booking.com, that lets you book all kinds of accommodations in Croatia.

Different types of accommodations have different rules about how to cancel and pay.

If you want to book an apartment or house in Croatia, Airbnb is the place to go. Many property owners prefer to list their home on Airbnb instead of Booking.com because Airbnb's fees are much cheaper. To use Airbnb, you'll need to make an account. It's not expensive. And if you use this link to make it, we'll give you 24€ to use on future trips.

MyIstria: is an online tour agency based in Istria that has a lot of villas in Croatia. As a new company, they only rented villas in Istria, which is where the name comes from. Now, their website has a lot of different houses for rent all over Croatia.

Excepedia: Excepedia is well known in Croatia. It does list vacation homes there, but most people use it to book hotels there. Expedia is a good option for people who want to book a flight and a room at the same time.

Web sites for tour operators: A lot of hotels in Croatia are sold through a large network of traditional tour operators and brick-and-mortar travel companies, such as Jet2Holidays and TUI UK (formerly Thomson). People coming from the UK can often get better deals through these businesses.

Website for the property: Many places to stay in Croatia, especially hotels, have their own websites. Always look at what they have to offer on their website and call the property directly to see if they have any straight deals.

Chapter 6: Top Attractions

Croatia is one of the most beautiful places in the world. Croatia has been at the meeting point of East and West for a very long time. Its borders and governments have changed many times in the past, and a lot of that history is painful.

But Croatia today is a celebration of life, energy, and natural beauty. The people are very friendly and helpful, and there are thousands and thousands of places to see.

Some of the best things to see and do in Croatia are its old towns and untouched nature. Some of the best museums, art galleries, restaurants, and shops in the country are in Zagreb, the country's lively capital city.

Along the shore, harbor towns that are hundreds of years old are full of stone buildings from the time of the Venetians. There are also many pebble beaches where you can do activities like windsurfing, water skiing, and scuba diving.

The beautiful islands of Croatia in the Adriatic are a haven for sailors and people who just want to relax and enjoy the Mediterranean sun.

Make sure you check out this list of the best things to see and do in Croatia so you can get the most out of your trip there.

1. Dubrovnik

It is known as "The Pearl of the Adriatic."

Dubrovnik is the most popular tourist location in Croatia and a UNESCO World Heritage site. The beautiful Old Town is surrounded by strong medieval walls that protect it.

To see the city's sights for the first time, you should start with a walk around the Old Town Walls. There are forts, towers, and cannons all along these strong old walls, which make up a two-kilometer circuit.

Keep in mind that tickets to walk along the walls cost a lot. However, for the same price as this one ticket, you can get a Dubrovnik Pass that lets you see many of the city's best sights.

While the walls are interesting, they're not the only thing to see and do in Dubrovnik. There is a lot of life in the Old Town; it feels like a movie set come to life. Having said that, it was the real sets of HBO's Game of Thrones and Star Wars: The Last Jedi that brought in so many tourists.

The famous Pile Gate, which was made in 1537 and is one of the most impressive buildings in the city, is probably how you'll get into the Old Town.

From the top of the walls, you can see the Adriatic Sea and the roofs of the Old Town in a beautiful way.

You can also have fun in Dubrovnik by walking along the Stradun, a 300-meter-long pedestrian street with shops, cafés, and restaurants. The Stradun is famous for its white limestone cobblestones.

The beautiful church, the famous Square of the Loggia with its beautiful old buildings and monuments, and Fort Lovrijenac, one of the country's most important fortresses are all things you shouldn't miss.

In case this sounds like too much praise, let me be honest: Dubrovnik is busy. It might be too crowded to say it is, especially if you go in the summer when a cruise ship is in port. It's going to be hard to get through the small streets, and parks aren't even going to be close.

Even with all the people, Dubrovnik still has the magic of a fairy story and is mesmerizing.

2. Diocletian's Palace in Split

Split is the second largest city in Croatia, after Zagreb. It was built inside the huge Roman walls of the Diocletian Palace (Dioklecijanovapalaca). It was built by the Roman Emperor Diocletian and has a view of the Adriatic Sea. He retired here in AD 305.

The palace is square, more like a castle than a palace, and it used to house the Emperor's personal guard. It has four huge gates, three of which can be reached from land and one of which used to open directly onto the water.

Inside the walls, you can see the beautiful Peristyle, which is a garden with arches, and the Cathedral of St. Domnius, which has an elegant bell tower.

Going to see the illuminated ruins at night is a fun thing to do. During the day, there are often bands and other events. Some people can only walk in the Old Town, which is a UNESCO World Heritage Site.

The southern gate of the city is the best way to get to the palace. It's the gate that stands in front of St. Dominic Church. The castle will be right on your left after you go through the gate.

Make sure you get there early. This is Split's main draw, and there are often too many people to handle. You should have the place (almost) all to yourself if you go to Croatia before June.

3. Plitvice Lakes National Park

The Plitvice Lakes National Park (Nacionalni park Plitvickajezera) is the most popular inland feature in Croatia. It has 16 emerald-blue lakes surrounded by steep, forested hills and linked by a series of thundering waterfalls.

The park, which was the country's first national park, is crossed by a network of trails and wooden bridges. The entrance fee includes boat rides on the lakes.

Because the park is so natural and lush, it is a safe home for wild animals like owls, falcons, wolves, and bears (though they are shy, so you probably won't see them).

If you want to spend the night, there are a number of hotels near the park. From Zagreb and Zadar, you can take a bus on a planned tour to see Plitvice.

If you want to go without a tour guide, make sure you book your tickets ahead of time. Over a million people come every year, making it a very popular tourist spot.

4. Hvar Island

A lot of people go to Croatia to see the beautiful Dalmatian islands. Hvar is the most popular of these islands. These are some of the best hotels and seafood places in the country. They are all in the cool city of Hvar.

The city's car-free Old Town dates back to when it was ruled by the Venetians (1420–1797). It has a large main square with a church from the 16th century, a pretty fishing harbor, and a fortress on top of a hill.

Yachters, famous people, and tourists who come to Hvar to enjoy its beaches and water sports all like it. From Split, you can take a boat there.

5. Korčula Island

The city of Korcula is the main village on the same-named island in South Dalmatia. It is tucked away on a small peninsula. It is protected by walls and towers from the Middle Ages, and the stone alleys are set up in a herringbone design to block the wind. There are many old, fancy stone buildings in Korcula that were made when the island was ruled by the Venetians.

One of the most interesting things to see is Marco Polo House, which is said to be where the famous explorer was born in the 1300s. Another great thing to do is see the moreska sword dance, a traditional dance that is put on for guests just outside the town walls every summer evening.

To really get into the spirit of Korcula, you can take a catamaran from Split (every day) or Dubrovnik (only in the summer) to the ancient town center.

6. Rovinj

The seaside town of Rovinj is in northwest Croatia, on the Istrian peninsula. It was built in the Venetian era and has pastel-colored houses that surround a pretty fishing harbor. A church on top of a hill with an elegant bell tower stands in the middle of the town.
The nearby sandy beaches aren't the main draw for tourists. The Batana Eco-Museum on the water tells the story of the batana, a type of wooden boat that local fishermen use. Plus, you can check out a lot of high-end hotels, fish restaurants, and art galleries.

Don't forget to check out the beaches near Rovinj either. You can read a book on these beautiful, quiet beaches and soak up the sun on the warm, white sand. Cisterna Beach, Cuvi Beach, and Skaraba Beach are some of nice spots in Rovinj.

People there speak a language that is a mix of Croatian and Italian. The airport that is closest is in Pula.

7. Gornji Grad in Zagreb

The ancient Gornji Grad (Upper Town) district is the best place to see in Zagreb. The cathedral, with its neo-Gothic front and twin steeples, the treasury, which has a large collection of religious art and artifacts, and the Croatian Parliament (Hrvatski sabor) are all famous tourist spots.

The famous colored tiles roof of the Church of St. Mark and the 13th-century Tower of Lotrscak are also worth seeing. You can climb the tower to get great views of the city and the area around it. The Museum of Broken Relationships is also a must-see that most people love.

8. Rijeka

Tourists to the Dalmatian Coast often miss the beautiful city of Rijeka, but you should definitely add it to your list of places to visit in Croatia.

Plus, there aren't as many people in this historically important port city, and there are lots of sights and things to do for people who do decide to go.

It was also a home base for tourists who wanted to see the northern coast of Croatia. They loved that Rijeka was easy to get to from Zagreb and that it was a great place to start exploring Istria.

But Rijeka is a place that you should visit, especially its Old Town. One of the best things to do is to walk along the well-kept cobblestone streets and roads that are lined with beautiful townhouses, homes, and old shops and businesses that were built in the 1700s.

9. Taking a boat tour of Kornati National Park

The Kornati island is 35 kilometers long and 13 kilometers wide, covering an area of about 320 square kilometers. It is made up of 89 small and large islets that are spread out in different directions.

The islets are mostly uninhabited, with only a few very basic stone houses scattered around. The land is dry and rocky, with little fertile soil. Local fishers and shepherds built them as one-room homes in the beginning, but now they're often used as vacation homes or seafood restaurants during the summer.

Taking a private sailing boat is the best way to see this incredibly beautiful coastal area. Biograd Na Moru is the closest charter base.

You can also take a pleasure boat from Zadar or Sibenik on the mainland to the Kornati for the day. If you're going to "sail under your own step," you'll need to buy a legal permit online.

10. Mljet National Park

A national park has been set up on the western third of the island of Mljet. It is mostly made up of dense forests and two linked turquoise saltwater lakes. One of the lakes has an islet with a Benedictine monastery from the 1100s that you can visit by taxi-boat.

Nature fans love the park because it has lots of things to do, like walking through the woods on one of the many paths that are there.

One more thing, there is a nine-kilometer trail that goes around the lakes and is great for walks or mountain biking. People also like to swim and do activities like kayaking (you can take kayaks to explore the lakes).

The island only has one hotel, but in the summer, local families give out rooms to tourists, and there are also a number of good campgrounds. From Dubrovnik, you can take a boat or a catamaran to get to Mljet.

11. Trogir

The charming seaside town of Trogir is often listed as one of the best places to visit on Croatia's beautiful Dalmatian coast. It's a great place to spend a holiday. Beginning in 380 BC, Trogir has a long and interesting past. It has been ruled by the Greeks, the Romans, the Hungarians, and the Venetians.

From the past of Old Town to the naturally beautiful beaches of Ciovo, the island across the water from Old Town, this city is a great place to live. The farmers market is also very nice, and there are lots of conveniences like grocery stores, exercise centers, and shopping.

12. Sibenik

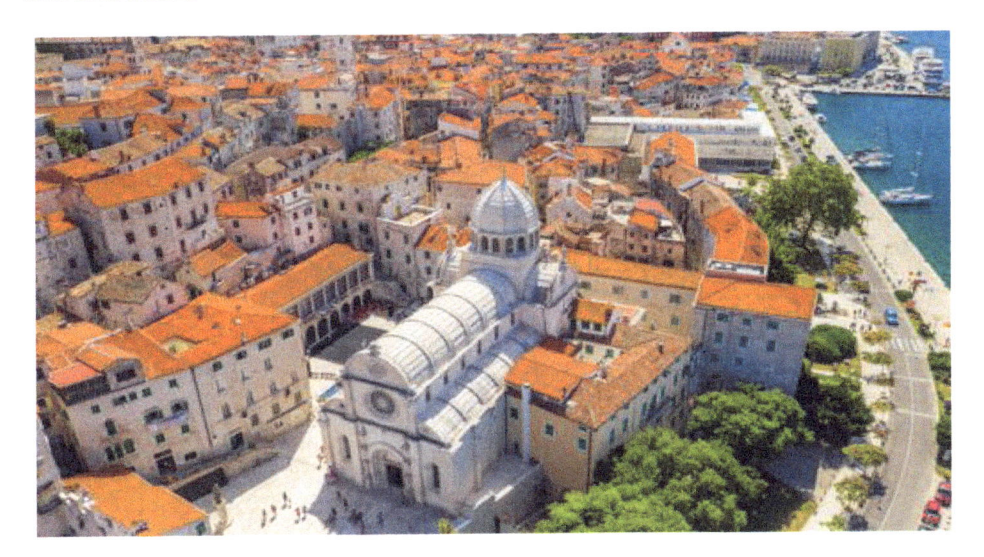

The historical city of Sibenik in Dalmatia has a lot to offer tourists to Croatia. Its past goes back to the 11th century and is very interesting to learn about.

There are lots of fun things to do here, and it's not always as busy as other popular spots in this lovely country.

First, check out the perfectly kept historic center of Old Town. There are many interesting things to see and beautiful buildings from the 15th and 16th centuries here. The Cathedral of St. James (KatedralaSv. Jakova), built in the 1400s, is one of the most beautiful churches in all of Croatia and is on the list of UNESCO World Heritage Sites.

Also worth seeing are the ruins of St. John's Fortress, which are high up on a hill overlooking the town and offering stunning views of the Adriatic Sea, and the equally important St. Michael's Fortress, which is known for the traditional shows held on its charming outdoor stage.

For many, the best thing about Sibenik is that, compared to places like Split and Dubrovnik, it still feels like a secret. The cute city on top of a hill has lots of small streets and hidden stairs to discover.

Along the water, bars are busy places where tourists and locals alike can grab a tasty meal. Azimut, a cafe, performance space, and studio on the river, is a popular spot for tourists to rest.

Chapter 7: Outdoor Activities and Nature

Hiking in Paklenica National Park

There are a lot of national parks near the town of Zadar in the middle of Croatia. South-East of the island is the beautiful Krka National Park, which has beautiful lakes and waterfalls.

The Zadar islands, which include Kornati National Park on Dugi Otok, are to the west. The beautiful Paklenica National Park is to the north of Zadar. It has rocky valleys, rough mountains, and lots of beautiful wildlife.

Many great things to do can be found in Paklenica National Park. One of the best is hiking. It's really simple to get from Zadar to Paklenica!

The best way to get to Paklenica National Park from Zadar

If you like climbing and being outside, Paklenica National Park is a great place to go. I'll show you the best ways to get from Zadar to Paklenica National Park below.

Take bus

Do this. It's really simple to take the bus from Zadar to Paklenica.

But you'll have to walk a lot more during the day. The bus will pick you up at the Zadar bus stop and drop you off at StarigradPaklenica. The early bus starts at 8 a.m. and gets there at 8:50 a.m.

It takes twenty minutes to walk from where you get off the bus to where the park starts. It's another 2 km walk to the canyon, which is where the real fun begins.

Drive

It's pretty easy to drive from Zadar to Paklenica. It shouldn't take more than 45 minutes.

There are two ways to get into the Park, and you'll have to pay to park when you get there. It will cost €2 a day for a small car and €4 a day for a minibus or other big car.

Entrance 2 (Mala Paklenica) will be closed if you are traveling during the off-season, so make sure you arrive through Entrance 1. The trails at Entrance 2 are also very difficult, so they are mostly only used by very experienced walkers.

Get a taxi

Need to get from Zadar to Paklenica but don't have a car or time to take the bus? Call a taxi. This costs about €100, but it could be a good choice for groups.

How to Spend Your Time in Paklenica National Park

There is so much wild beauty in Paklenica National Park. It really takes your breath away. It doesn't matter if you only stay for an afternoon or for several days. There is plenty to do in the park.

Hiking in Paklenica National Park

One of the most popular things to do in Paklenica National Park is to go hiking.

You can hike or bike on about 175 km of paths, which should keep you busy for a while. With a height of 1757 meters, VaganskiVrh is the highest point in Paklenica.

At the park's entrance, the paths are marked with information about how long they are, how long they take, and how hard they are. This is also where you can buy a map.

No matter which path you choose, the views are stunning. Trails that last less than an hour are good for people who have never been skiing before. There are also trails that will test even the most skilled walkers.

The path to the Paklenica Mountain hut is the most-used trail from Entrance 1. If you don't stop, this will take about two hours. Of course, it will take two more hours to get back to the beginning.

The trail goes through the beautiful Velika Paklenica Canyon, which has some amazing views.

Visit some Caves

Paklenica National Park has a few caves. Manita Peñ cave is the only one that is open to the public, though.

It's about 1.5 km to the cave from the park gate, and it takes about 30 minutes to look around inside. A €5 ticket can be bought at the cave's entrance.

In the caves' large rooms, you can see a lot of interesting animals, like insects and different kinds of bats.

Climbing

Paklenica National Park is a great place to climb! One of the best places to climb in Croatia and Europe is the Velika Paklenica Canyon.

Over 5,000 climbers of all ages and skill levels visit every year because there are about 500 well-equipped routes. You can also rent the gear if you need to.

Taking pictures of nature in Paklenica National Park

Paklenica National Park is a must-see for people who love taking pictures. In the park, there are more than 1,000 plant species and more than 59 mouse types.

The rocks are also very different, and there are two very dramatic canyons and two beautiful pine woods.

Paklenica National Park Restaurants And Accommdations

The park of Paklenica has a few mountain huts. They're great places to get food or drinks.

You will be greeted with a free shot of Rakia and then be able to enjoy some wonderful, authentic food and a conversation with the owner, who is very charming.

The same path leads to the Paklenica Mountain Lodge as well. There are, however, better views from RamicaDvori, which makes the extra walk well worth it.

Exhibition of an Underground Bunker

During the 1950s, when things were bad between Yugoslavia and the Soviet Union, the army built these bunkers. Until the 1990s, no one knew about them.

They are now a place where people can learn about the past of the area.

Ethno Houses

The hamlet of Marasovici has an ethno house and a bar. It is only open to tourists during the summer. There are a few mills from the 1800s close to Entrance 1. These don't work anymore, but they've been fixed up and are now open during the busy season.

When Is The Best Time To Hike In Paklenica National Park?

You can visit Paklenica National Park at any time of the year. As was already said, during the winter only Entrance 1 is open. Because the park is close to the water, the weather isn't as bad as it could be further inland.

This means that you can go to the park any time of the year. In the summer, it does get crowded, but not as much as other National Parks in the area.

Come in March. The weather will be nice, so it will work out great for you. This place is great to visit in early spring or mid- to late-autumn.

How Long Can You Stay in the Park?

A park pass can be bought for one, three, or five days. If you plan to stay in the area for a while, you can also buy a yearly pass. If you stay for a few days, there is plenty to see. A full day can be spent there. You can take a slow walk and eat lunch at one of the mountain huts. You can do this as a day trip from Zadar, which is close by.

If you want to stay longer, you should know that you can't sleep in the park. You can, however, camp in the nearby towns or stay the night in one of the parks' Mountain Lodges.

Cost to get into Paklenica National Park

Adult tickets cost different amounts at different times of the year. In March, a day in the park cost €6. You can buy tickets online or at the door. Make sure you keep your ticket with you all day in case the staff needs to see it.

The machine might not work, but you can still pay with a card. If you stop in the mountain huts or the cave, you will also need cash. It is a good idea to bring cash. Keep in mind that Croatia now uses the Euro.

Is it safe to hike in Paklenica National Park?

It's safe to go hiking in Paklenica. When going anywhere, it's important to remember these safety tips:

- Always stay on the trails that have been marked.
- Try not to go hiking by yourself.
- Land mines were set up during the wars in the 1990s, and some may still be there in remote places. On the boards at the entrance, the mountain trails that have been cleared of mines are marked.
- Tell someone where you're going in case you get lost.
- Check the weather before you leave.
- Pack things correctly
- You can't ride a bike in the park, and dogs need to be on a leash to protect the animals.
- If you need help right away, call 112.
- There are bathrooms at the park's entrance. This isn't really a safety problem, but it's good to know.

What to Bring to Paklenica National Park for a Day Hike

Below is a simple list of things to bring on a day hike in Paklenica National Park.

- 2 Shoes or boots for hiking
- A backpack
- Euros in cash
- Snacks for the hike
- A water bottle with at least one liter of water in the summer. A few pints will let you fill up on the way.
- Clothes that are right for the weather, like a windbreaker, climbing socks, a buff or hat, and fleece. If you want to go further on your hike, make sure to wear clothes so that you can adapt to changing weather.
- Good insecticide
- Sunscreen and eyes protection (sunglasses)
- Map or a GPS or map app that you downloaded to your phone
- Phone
- A good camera with lots of memory for taking pictures of the beautiful scenery

It will be a great day of climbing in Paklenica National Park, and the trip from Zadar will be well worth it. Being close to nature will make you feel calm, peaceful, and at ease.

Going Sailing Or Boating Along The Coast Of Dalmatia

The Dalmatian Coast in Croatia might be the most beautiful shoreline, and it's also one of the best places in Croatia to visit different islands. There are rough rocks on the land that meets the sea, and along the coast, there are dozens of pretty islands. There are good reasons why so many people love sailing vacations in Croatia.

Why Sail in Croatia's Dalmatian Coast?

The beautiful water is one reason. The water along the Dalmatian coast is warm, clear, and warm, making it a great place to swim and boat. The Adriatic is a beautiful stretch of water. The dramatic shoreline also makes for a beautiful background. Instead of seeing nothing but the open sea, you can see the water framed by dramatic headlands and rocky island silhouettes.

The beautiful islands and cute seaside towns that are spread out along the Dalmatian Coast are another reason to go there. The area has a lot of different things to offer, from peaceful national parks to hotspots for famous people. Some of my favorite places are the ones that aren't as busy, like small towns with red roofs and fishing villages where you can enjoy Croatia's still beauty.

The great food is a third reason. The best thing about Croatia for me was the fish. In a quiet harbor, there's nothing better than having fish dinner straight from the sea.

Seven Beautiful Places To Stop While Sailing Along The Dalmatian Coast

1. Split

Split is a good place to start a sailing vacation in Croatia. An international airport is here, and a lot of small ship trips and sailing flotillas leave from here.

There are bars by the harbor where you can relax before getting on the boat and watch the many boats arrive if you get there a few hours before the departure time.

It's more than just a place to start, though. People from many different times have loved Split, which is the second-largest city in Croatia. The Greeks built this city in the second or third century BC, and in 305 AD, the Roman Emperor Diocletian built a house here for himself to live in. The beautiful white stone structure of Diocletian's Palace is now a Unesco World Heritage Site. You should see it before or after you set sail. You might want to take a tour of Diocletian's Palace and Split's old town.

2. Hvar

Hvar island is the most beautiful place in Croatia. A lot of the wealthy people like to hang out in Hvar Town. There are superyachts and maybe even a star or two in this pretty harbor town with a fortress on top of a hill and views of the pretty Paklinksi islands.

Because of this, Hvar has fancier hotels and restaurants, and prices are higher generally.

Even so, Hvar didn't feel exclusive or out of reach for regular people. The town is lovely to walk around, and there are a number of peaceful, rocky coves near the town where you can enjoy the water.

There are lots of things to do there. It's possible to walk up to Hvar Fortress, which has great views of the harbor. Lots of people also like to take tours of the Paklinski islands. You can also just chill out in one of the many bars or restaurants in and around St. Stephen's Square and take in the atmosphere.

There is more beauty and a little less glitz elsewhere on Hvar Island. Stari Grad's main town is also beautiful, but not as busy as Hvar Town. It is in a natural bay that is protected, and there is another castle and a Dominican monastery here.

The best way for tourists to see a popular part of the island is from the water. Sućuraj is a town on the eastern end of Hvar island. The Sućuraj lighthouse is at the very top of the hill and faces east. It looks so small next to the huge mountains on the shore; it was a great place to take a picture.

3. Korčula

On the island of Korčula, one of Croatia's most famous protected towns, a walled citadel, stands proudly out into the sea. You wish you had a drone to take pictures of it from above, like so many Instagram shots.

From the 1400s on, Korčula Town has been a car-free zone. It's fun to walk around the marble streets and arched alleys and pretend you've gone back in time several hundred years.

There is a museum about Marco Polo, who is said to have been born in Korčula. During the summer, traditional sword dance shows happen twice a week. You can look around the towers and city walls. A ladder leads up to an open-air bar in one of the towers. It's small, but definitely a one-of-a-kind spot to sip a drink!

If you want to see more of the coast, the hop-on-hop-off boat is a great option. From the walls or the small dock area just outside the walls, you can also see beautiful sunsets over the channel of water between the island and the shore.

4. Makarska

Makarska is a lively beach town that is about 90 km south of Split.

It has a busy harbor (marina), a colorful central square and market, and many places with terraces and ice cream stands where you can eat outside. Biokovo National Park is full of things to do on the water and in the woods. You can even go skywalking there. A lot of people think that Makarska is popular, but not too crowded with tourists.

The pebble beach with plants along it is the best part, though. Since it faces west, it's a great spot to watch the sun go down.

5. Trstenik

Trstenik is a quiet fishing village on the Pelješac peninsula. The only things that are there are an eatery, a small harbor, and a beach with rocks.

In this place you caneat some of the best fish in croatia. At the diner by the harbor, you can order tasty food while sitting on the dock.

6. Dubrovnik

Any trip to the Dalmatian Coast should start and end in Dubrovnik. It's not Croatia's only walled town, but it's the biggest and most impressive. The old town is a maze of buildings with red roofs and baroque churches with domes. The city walls and towers make up the outside of the old town. Its streets are made of shiny marble that sparkles in the evening light, which is how it got the name "Pearl of the Adriatic."

It is also where the TV show Game of Thrones filmed King's Landing.

In the 9th century, there was a fortified town here. The walls that are still there today were built in the 13th century. The walls go all the way around the city, which is a great thing to do because you'll get to see the sea, the islands nearby, the harbor, and the city itself from many angles.

There is a lot to see inside the walled city during the day, including the beautiful main street, Stradun. This long, wide marble walkway is grand and beautiful. In the 1990s, the Yugoslav war did some damage to Dubrovnik. In the old town, there is a photography show about that war that you can learn more about.

You can rent boats near the Pile Gate if you want to do something more active. You can do this and boat around Lokrum island, which is close by. When the boats come and go from Dubrovnik harbor, crossing the channel can be a little scary. But once you get to the island, it's very peaceful and beautiful.

There are many places to choose from in the evening, and some of them have views of the water. Walk around the old town's small streets as it gets dark. It's very safe and very romantic at night.

But you can enjoy the sunset from the top of the city walls, close to the Minceta tower. Many people have said it's one of the most beautiful spots to watch the sun go down. From this spot, the red roofs of the city will glow in the warm light of the setting sun. It works like magic.

Not sure whether to spend your time in Split or Dubrovnik? Both are great, but Dubrovnik is the city that most tourists love.

7. Mljet Island

The long, thin island of Mljet is known for its national park and beautiful nature. On the west side of the island, in the National Park, there are two saltwater lakes that are easy to get to from Pomena, the harbor town.

The lakes with trees around them have clear blue water, especially Malo Jezero, which is the smaller of the two. The smaller lake has a walk around it, and the bigger lake, Veliko Jezero, has boats that you can use to cross it. You will be taken by boat to a very small islet (it's really an island within an island!). There is a Benedictine monastery from the 1200s on this islet.

Since there is now a restaurant on the island, you don't have to spend money to enjoy it. You can also just sit by the calm water if you'd rather.

Chapter 8: Scuba diving

Croatia has a lot to offer tourists, and diving is one of those fun things to do.

In the 1950s, a lot of people came here to do different water sports and learn about the underwater world. This could be your next best trip if you think about how lively and interesting it is.

Remember that the best diving school in the area is close to the villas you can rent for your vacation. This is a big plus for anyone who likes swimming, whether they want to snorkel or scuba dive.

Along with the delicious food in Istria, Croatia has something else that makes it stand out. You can dive in some of the best places in the Adriatic Sea from here. It has more than 1,000 islands.

This means that if you go diving in Croatia, you can see many rocks, caverns, tunnels, and other natural features. And the best thing about swimming in Croatia is that you can see beautiful plants and animals.

In general, you can swim in Croatia all year long. It is a great place to go swimming in Europe, especially from April to November. In fact, there are a lot of tourists in the summer, but the warm water and sunshine will make you forget about your troubles.

During the summer, the air temperature is mostly between 17 and 35 degrees Celsius, and the water temperature is a nice 27 degrees Celsius.

Keep in mind that the depth of the water and how close it is to freshwater streams can change its temperature. We know from experience, though, that it won't bother you. During the winter, the water temperature could drop as low as 10 degrees Celsius and the air temperature could drop to 5 to 15 degrees Celsius. Also, you might want to know that May, June, October, and November are the months with the most rain.

In other words, you will find the best conditions for diving, swimming, or scuba diving in Croatia.

There are many diving schools right next to villas that you can rent, as well as other services like restaurants and boat tours. Additionally, the best thing about diving in Croatia is that in the summer you can enjoy a breathtaking view from 30 meters below.

No matter what time of year it is, this country is the best place to get qualified in a dry suit. Also, keep in mind that you can only dive in Croatia if you have a pass from the Croatian Diving Federation. Divers who are qualified can get one for about 15 euros and keep it for a year.
You will need to show proof of a certification card and visa in order to get one.

Dive around the famous shipwrecks in Istria

Istria is one of the best places in Croatia to go swimming. From our own experience, we can say that the underwater world here will make you speechless. Istria is mostly suggested for divers of all types, even those who have never been diving before.

You can trust the Shark Diving Center more than any other in the area, so a diving trip to Istria could be the best time of your life.

You can make the most of your trip to Croatia by renting one of the houses close to the diving center.

Pula

People love to swim in Istria, and Pula city is one of the best places to do it. The wreck of an admiral ship can be seen here. It is 20 to 34 meters deep and is close to the shore. And because this is a family-friendly and dog-friendly area (with dog-friendly beaches), you will have access to many great features, such as private pools at your accommodations and great restaurants in the area.

Medulin

Medulin is another great place to dive in Istria. Since both are close to Pula, you can see them both in one trip. You can also get anything you might need for snorkeling or scuba diving at the Shark diving school, which is right there. All around the water in Medulin, there are a lot of famous shipwrecks and beautiful underwater caves.

Rovinj and Porec

There is diving in Porec and Rovinj that might be a great choice for people who like to try new things or are expert divers. Divers are always interested in Banjol Island, which is in front of Rovinj's old town. This is especially true in the summer.

And here's a secret: if you go swimming in Porec, you can meet the beautiful seahorses that live in the water around Istria.

The Baron Gautsch wreck in Rovinj should be on your list of places to dive. It's about 40 meters deep and one of the most beautiful bodies of water in Croatia. Remember that this is only a good place to dive for experienced and advanced divers.

Snorkeling

Some of the best snorkeling spots in Europe are in Croatia. Snorkeling is a great way to see the beautiful undersea world.

Crystal-clear waters, a wide range of sea life, and stunning beaches make Croatia a dream place for snorkelers.

Croatia has more than 6,000 kilometers of beautiful shoreline and more than 1,200 islands, islets, and reefs that make up its diverse marine ecosystems. There are many chances to snorkel there.

From colorful coral reefs to peaceful underwater caves, these amazing places are great for exploring in their own way. No matter how much you know about snorkeling or how new you are, Croatia's beautiful underwater world will leave you with memories that you will never forget.

Chapter 9: What to expect: why snorkeling in Croatia is a good idea

There are many great reasons to go snorkeling in Croatia. Here are some good things that will happen while you explore its beautiful watery world.

- Water that is clean and clear
- Very good vision underwater
- Lots of sea life
- Shipwrecks, caves, and islands under the water
- Safe ways to swim
- Activity that is cheap and easy to get to
- Warm weather
- Beautiful Islands and Coast
- Experience the Culture

1. Clean water

If you go snorkeling in Croatia, you will be amazed by the crystal clear seas that the country is known for. The European Environment Agency's yearly bathing water report always puts Croatia in the top five European countries. More than 95% of its coastal bathing sites are rated as having excellent water quality.

2. Very good underwatervisibility

Croatia's waters are so clear that you can see everything, which makes it a great place to go diving. You can see the different kinds of sea life clearly and without any problems. Along the coast, the Adriatic Sea is up to 30 meters (100 ft) clear, which makes it a great place to see things beneath.

There are small rocks on the bottom, especially in the shallow water, which makes the water clearer. It's also clear because of the karst coast and the small amount of rivers. The Adriatic Sea is a great place to swim, fish, and take pictures underwater.

3. Diverse Marine Life

The Adriatic Sea has a lot of different kinds of sea life, even though it is pretty small and only partly protected. Over 7,000 plant and animal types live there, and more than 500 of them are unique to the area.

The Mediterranean feather star is a great example because it has lived and grown in these waters for over 500 million years.

There are over 300 species of fish, 240 species of shellfish, 800 species of snails, and many other interesting crabs, echinoderms, and other animals that live in the Adriatic.

The Adriatic Sea is a great place to snorkel because there is a lot of interesting sea life to see. There are many beautiful things in the ocean world, from colorful fish and graceful sea turtles to interesting creatures like starfish, octopuses, and jellyfish.

It is interesting to note that the bottlenose, striped, and common dolphins all live in the Adriatic Sea. The beautiful island of Losinj is one of the most interesting places to see these dolphins. In Croatia, you can even adopt a dolphin!

Many kinds of fish, like sea bass, sea bream, striped bream, white seabream, john dory, sand smelt, garfish, and more, may be in the water with you while you swim in Croatia. You're about to see a beautiful marine environment that will blow your mind.

4. Shipwrecks, caves, cliffs, reefs, and corals all under the water

People love the Adriatic Sea for its variety of sea life and interesting ships, caves, crags, and reefs. No one knows how many shipwrecks there are in the Adriatic Sea in Croatia, but Croatian diver and author Danijel Frka wrote a book called "The Sunken Treasure of the Adriatic Sea" that lists 75 shipwrecks, fighter planes that have sunk, and old sites.

You can explore and learn about a different side of the Adriatic by going to these ships. Baron Gautsch, near Rovinj, is one of the most famous passenger shipwrecks in Croatia. It is now a popular place to dive where many marine species live.

Sponge fish, groupers, and red mullets now live in the wreck of the Taranto ship, which sunk near Dubrovnik. There are many ancient amphorae on the seabed on the northwest side of Vis Island. This shows that Vis was an important trade hub in the past.

Along the karst coast of Croatia, there are many underwater caves, pits, holes, crags, rocks, and walls. There are also shipwrecks. There are red gorgonians, corals, sardines, moray eels, groupers, and monkfish living in the Bijelac Cliff near Lastovo. The cliff is made up of unique cleft and limestone rocks.

Mali and VelikiĆutin are two underwater rocks and caves on the eastern side of Cres Island that are famous for the bright red gorgonians, rare yellow fan corals, and lots of different kinds of fish.

Croatia has a lot of coral formations, most of which can be found on the islands' outer shores.

The pillow coral that is only found in the Mediterranean is the biggest coral reef in the area. It can be found in the Great Lake of Mljet Island, which is 4 to 18 meters deep.

The pink color of this beautiful coral reef is very appealing. For those looking for a beautiful sight, the Kampanel spot on Vodnjak, the westernmost island of Hvar's Pakleni Otok, is a great place to see the beauty of gorgonian corals, even just above the water.

5. Safe Ways to Snorkel

Snorkeling and swimming fans can feel safe and enjoy themselves in the Adriatic Sea. You can be sure that there are no dangerous animals in these waters. Still, it's always a good idea to be careful and follow safety rules when doing anything in or near water.

People have told stories about seeing sharks in the Adriatic, but they are not really a threat. It is very rare to see these beautiful mammals, and no attacks on people have been reported in Croatian waters.

In the Adriatic, you may see fireworms, spiderfish, jellyfish, and stingrays more often, but not very often. It is important to remember that these animals are not directly dangerous to people, but their defenses can hurt and bother people. Snorkelers in Croatia are still most worried about stepping on a sea urchin.

Rest assured that the Adriatic Sea has a beautiful underwater world that you can explore. You will be safe and have a great time as you enjoy its beauty.

6. Cheap and accessible

Not only is snorkeling in Croatia cheap, but it's also easy for everyone to get to. You can dive into the Adriatic Sea and see what it has to offer with just a mask, snorkel, and fins.

You can still swim in Croatia, even if you don't have the money to buy the gear. There are some restrictions, though.

You can actually do this, even though your eyes might feel a little burned and you might not be able to see as well as when you're wearing a mask.

Croatia is a great place to go diving because everyone is welcome to enjoy the beautiful Adriatic Sea.

Also, Croatia has reasonable prices for tours and renting gear, and you can get to many places by boat or right from the shore. Also, the country's many islands and seaside towns make it easy to get to great snorkeling spots.

Also, Croatia has a wide range of places to stay, from high-end hotels to cozy flats and villas, so there is something for everyone.

A lot of tour companies also offer cheap deals that include lodging and snorkeling activities. This makes it a great vacation choice for families or people traveling alone who want to save money.

7. Warm Weather

The warm weather in the Adriatic Sea makes it a great place to explore underwater. The normal water temperature in the summer is about 25 degrees Celsius (79 degrees Fahrenheit), which makes snorkeling comfortable and fun.

8. Coast and islands that look beautiful

The shoreline of Croatia is almost 6,000 km long, which includes islands. This makes it a great place to go snorkeling.

Every island and town on the coast has its own special charm, with beaches, coves, and views that will take your breath away.

9. Experience the Culture

When you snorkel in Croatia, you can see more than just the sea. The architecture, food, and traditions of the country show that it has a long and interesting past. You can go snorkeling and then visit historical places, traditional villages, and real local restaurants at the same time.

These are the eight best places to snorkel in Croatia.

The clear waters of the Adriatic Sea cover the whole coast of Croatia. They show a rich underwater world that snorkelers can easily reach and doesn't cost a lot of money. And no matter where your travels take you in Croatia, you'll find beautiful places to explore the stunning underwater world.

I have carefully chosen eight amazing snorkeling spots in Croatia so that you can have a unique experience. I chose these places because of their beautiful nature scenery, interesting marine life, and amazing rock formations. I also thought about things like how easy it was to get to, how well the area was developed for tourists, and whether there were organized snorkeling trips that would make the experience smooth and complete.

Chapter 10: These are the eight best places in Croatia to swim

- The Brijuni National Park
- The Kamenjak Cape
- HvarisIan
- The coast of Makarska
- Vis Island
- Ducho Otok
- Veli Drevnik
- Island of Mljet

1. The National ParkBrijuni

Eight national parks are in Croatia. Brijuni is one of them. It is on the south coast of Istria.

The islands that make up the Brijuni National Park are called an archipelago. Brijuni is a great place to snorkel because it's one of the few places where you can go on an organized tour of underwater archaeological sites.

Along those lines, fishing near the Brijuni Islands has been tightly controlled since 1983, when it was made a national park.

Because of this, the underwater plants and animals in this area are incredibly well-preserved and plentiful when compared to other places. There are many kinds of sea urchins, crustaceans, shellfish, sponges, and fish living on the bottom. The pen-shell and the date-shell are also protected species that lucky viewers may be able to see. Keep your eyes open, because dolphins sometimes swim in the water around Brijuni.

How to Get There

From the village of Fazana, boats go to the Brijuni Islands. Between June and September, boats run every hour from 9:00 am to 10:00 pm.

You can make your own plans to swim around the island.

2. The Cape Kamenjak

Cape Kamenjak is a beautiful wildlife park that you should check out. It is at the southernmost point of Istria, close to Pula. This park is great if you like swimming, snorkeling, diving, long walks in nature, riding, or water sports like kayaking, windsurfing, or swimming. The park costs 15€ a day to enter for a car and its owner.

The coastline is mostly made up of rocky outcroppings, but there are also some pebble beaches with big, round rocks.

There are also interesting underwater caves near these shores. The Mediterranean monk seal lives in these caves. It is one of the most threatened mammals in the world. If you're lucky, you might see one while swimming in the water near Cape Kamenjak.

Dive into the clear blue water and explore the many underwater caves and tunnels that are full of different kinds of marine life.

How to Get to Cape Kamenjak

From Pula, go to Banjole and Premantura and follow the signs. Take a right turn toward Kamenjak when you get to the village of Premantura. It takes another two to three minutes to get to the park's gate.

3. Hvar Island

Croatia's Hvar Island is a popular summer vacation spot known for its lively nightlife and beautiful beaches. In addition to the lively mood of Hvar town, there are many outdoor activities, such as snorkeling, that can be done.

Two great places to swim on Hvar Island are the Pakleni Islands and the Red Rocks.

Just off the coast of Hvar Town are the Pakleni Islands, which have beautiful beaches, secret bays, and clear blue water that make them one of the most popular places to snorkel in Hvar.

People who come can also enjoy bars, beach clubs, and great restaurants. On the Pakleni Islands, Mlini Bay on Marinkovac Island and Perna Beach on Sveti Klement Island are both great places to swim. Kampanel on Vodnjak Island is a beautiful place to dive with lots of red gorgonians.

Red Rocks are rough rocks on the southern coast of Hvar Island that are famous for being a deep red color and a great place to snorkel.

Underwater, there are sea caves, tubes, and lots of different kinds of colorful sea life. For the best view of Red Rocks, take a boat tour or rent a kayak.

How to Get There

From Hvar port, you can take a taxi boat to get to the Paklinski Islands. Before 10 a.m., if you want to get a good spot on any of the beaches, you should get there.

A ticket to Pakleni Islands that goes both ways costs 10€. You could also take a boat and spend the day going between the islands, stopping to swim and snorkel along the way.

From the shore of Hvar, you can also join a number of guided kayaking and snorkeling tours.

A boat trip from Hvar Island is the best way to get to Red Rocks.

4. Makarska Riviera

If you like swimming, you have to go to the Makarska Riviera.

From Brela to Gradac, this stretch of coast is about 60 km long and has many great places to swim. People love the Makarska Riviera because it has cute coastal towns, pebbly beaches, and turquoise waters that are as clear as glass.

To see everything, you might want to rent a boat or go on a tour to get to beaches and spots that aren't easy to get to. Nugal Beach is famous for its clear waters and rocks, but you can only get there by boat or on foot.
The wild beaches between Drasnice and Igrani are a great place to relax. People say that Punta Rata Beach in Brela is one of the best beaches in Europe.

You can swim and see a lot of sea life, like sand smelt, sardines, groupers, and more.

In addition to swimming, there are many other fun things to do in the area. You could go camping in Biokovo Nature Park or visit nearby islands like Hvar and Brac to make your trip more interesting.

How to Get Around

The towns along the Makarska Riviera are very well connected by bus, so getting around is easy at any time of the day.
Taking the bus is an easy way to get around and see the area.

If you want to try something more exciting, you could rent a boat and go exploring the Riviera's beautiful bays and hidden beaches.
Instead, taking a car lets you find beaches that aren't as popular, showing off the real beauty of the area.

There are organized kayaking trips that can take you to some of the less well-known beaches that would be hard to get to otherwise if you're looking for a unique and immersive experience.

5. Vis Island

Vis Island is the most remote populated island in Croatia. Its natural beauty, open seas, and farthest location make it the best place to snorkel in Croatia.

On Vis Island, the best places to swim are Stiniva and Srebrna Beach, Ceska Villa Peninsula, the water around the Green Cave on Ravnik Island, Monk Seal Cave on Bisevo Island, and the Blue Lagoon on Budikovac Island. Vis also has old military sea caves that were used as shelters for ships during war. The diving spots are also fun to check out.

Vis was off-limits to foreign tourists from 1950 to 1989 because it was an important military base. This helped the island stay in such great shape. Today, Vis attracts tourists with its realness, beautiful environment, tasty food, and high-quality wine.

How to Get There

A high-speed boat from Split to Vis Island is the best way to get there. There is also a direct boat link between Vis and Hvar. There are also many day trips you can book from Split and Hvar to Vis.

6. Mljet Island

Mljet Island is in the Mediterranean Sea and has the biggest coral reef in the area, making it a great place for snorkeling fans.

In fact, the island is known as the greenest island in Croatia because it has untouched pine woods, beautiful beaches, and calm lakes.

The most beautiful thing about Mljet is its big national park, which covers the whole northwest part of the island. As a protected natural area, the park controls and limits all water activities, such as fishing. This makes for a healthy environment below the water.

The sea is clear and clean, and it is full of sea creatures like sea urchins, cucumbers, and an amazing variety of underwater hills, crags, and rocks.

Snorkeling is popular on the island at Veliko Jezero (Big Lake), Rikavica, and Odysseus Caves, which are full of sea creatures like sponges, octopuses, scorpionfish, and many types of small fish, crabs, and anemones.

How to Get There

You can take a boat from either Dubrovnik or Prapratno. You could also take a guided boat tour from Dubrovnik to Mljet.

7. Dugi Otok

For snorkeling fans, Dugi Otok is the best place to go. It's the northernmost island in the Zadar group.

There are many bays, beaches, and the beautiful Telascica Nature Park on the island. There is a lot of life underwater near Dugi Otok. This is partly because Telascica Nature Park and Kornati National Park are protected places where fishing is strictly controlled.

The island has a lot of great places to swim, like Lagnici Cliffs, which are in the northern part of the island near Veli Rat lighthouse.

The shipwreck of the Michele, which ran aground in 1983 and is now home to many fish and even some coral walls, can be explored here.

Brbiscica Cave, which is on the west coast of the island, is another great place to visit. This cave underwater is a unique place to swim because the sun's rays change the color of the water in a beautiful way. There are many kinds of fish that you can see here.

Finally, Telascica Bay is in the southern part of the island. It is a big natural bay with pine and oak woods, 6 islets, and a few small coves. One side of the bay has high cliffs.

It's a great place to snorkel because there are more than 250 sea creatures and over 300 plants living beneath. You can look at red coral and sponges that eat meat, as well as small fish, crabs, and octopuses.

How to Get Here

From the port of Zadar, ferry boats leave a few times a day. The Jadrolinija car boat is worth a look if you are traveling by car. The G&V Line can also take you to the island. People can take a boat to Sali. From Jadrolinija, you can take the car boat to Brbinj or the catamaran to Bozava. It takes about an hour and a half to cross.

8. Split

There are a lot of great places to swim near Split. Even though Kasjuni is the best place to snorkel in the city, more snorkelers go to two other places close. The Blue Lagoon is on the island of Drvenik Veli, which is near Trogir, and the Necujam Bay is on the island of Solta.

The Blue Lagoon is in a beautiful cove that is ringed by three islands. These are Drvenik Veli, Small Krknjasi, and Big Krknjasi. The cove is widely known as Krknjasi in the area.

With its bright blue and turquoise water and sandy bottom, the sea forms a beautiful underwater world full of sea urchins, octopuses, small crabs, and different Adriatic fish. From noon to 5 pm, tour boats that leave from Split and Trogir often spend the afternoons in the bay.

Before and after these times, the area changes into a peaceful, almost empty haven.

The shipwreck Kontesa is in the Necujam Bay on Solta Island. It has become one of the best places in Croatia to swim. You may not get the chance to swim near a shipwreck very often. Most shipwrecks are in deep water, so you need to know how to dive to explore them. But the Kontesa, a commercial ship that sunk a little more than ten years ago, is in shallow water and can be reached by anyone.

Besides the shipwreck, Necujam Bay has beautiful scenery that makes it worth a visit. One of the cool things about this place is that a man sells mojitos from his boat.

How to Get There

You can get to Split by car, bus, boat, plane, or train, among other ways. Split is the second-largest city in Croatia.
It is in the middle of the country and is an important transportation hub that links many local and foreign destinations.

But if you want to go to Blue Lagoon or Necujam Bay, you'll need to carefully plan how you'll get there. Four times a day, from June to September, a boat leaves from Trogir for Blue Lagoon. On Sundays and holidays, the ferry only leaves once a day.

In the summer, there are six daily boat trips from Split to Rogač, and in the winter, there are four daily trips. You'll still need to plan a way to get from Rogac to Necujam Bay, though.

Taking one of the organized boat tours from Trogir or Split is the best and fastest way to get to the islands.

Chapter 11: Tips on How to Snorkel in Croatia

Keep these tips in mind if you want to get the most out of your swimming trip in Croatia.

Pick the right time

In Croatia, the best time to swim is from June to September, when the weather is nice and the water is warm. If you want to swim in peace, don't go between July and August, when a lot of people are there.

Bring along your equipment

There are many shops and stands on Croatian beaches that sell snorkeling gear, but bringing your own will make sure that it fits well and is comfy. In the shops around here, a snorkeling set with a mask, snorkel, and fins costs about 35 €.

You should still bring your diving gear with you, though. Most kayaking and boat tours give you masks that fit everyone, but it's always better to have gear that fits you right.

Go along with water shoes

Do keep in mind that most of Croatia's beaches are rocky or pebbly. So, water shoes are recommended for comfort and ease of going in the water.
Water shoes are easy to find at stands and shops along the beach. They usually cost around 10 €. But if you buy them ahead of time, you can be sure to get the style you want.

Respect the environment

While snorkeling, if you're not careful, you might hurt marine life. Pay attention to what's going on around you and don't touch or hurt coral reefs or other animals.

Be careful

Always swim with someone else, and pay attention to what's going on around you. Before you go, check the weather, and stay away from areas with strong currents or bad visibility.

Rafting and kayaking in the Zrmanja River

The River Zrmanja is in the northern part of Dalmatia, near Velebit Mountain. It springs under the Poštak mountain in the southern part of Lika, which is in the middle of Croatia, and flows into the Novigrad Sea 12 kilometers from Obrovac.

It is 69 kilometers long, and since it is close to the water, you can go swimming there any time of the year.

The mountains and waterfalls along the Zrmanja make it one of the most beautiful rivers in Croatia, and it will take your breath away.

Its waters are very clear and flow through a tunnel that is about 200 meters deep. Many limestone waterfalls have been formed by the river in this area, but the 11-meter-high Veliki Buk waterfall stands out. Zrmanja rapids and paddling up the Krupa River is a great way to see beautiful scenery and have an exciting time.

These are two of the most beautiful rivers in Croatia and all of Europe.
You can kayak or raft on the Zrmanja River, which is tucked away in the countryside near Zadar. The river's clean water and untouched nature will amaze you.

Because the water is perfectly clear and warm, there is a beautiful tunnel and beautiful waterfalls. You will see a lot of fish and birds along the way, and you can check out live travertine waterfalls, which are a common karst feature.

The kayaking and rafting trip on the Zrmanja River starts in the town of Kastel Zegarski, which is an hour's drive from Zadar, an hour and a half from Sibenik, two hours from Split, and one hour and a half from the Plitvice Lakes Area.

No matter what kind of rafting experience you have, you will still enjoy it. In fact, this whitewater boating is safe enough for kids as young as 6. Even if you are an expert rafter, you will still enjoy it.

Besides the beautiful views we already talked about, you will also face more difficult rapids and drops that will give you a much-needed adrenaline rush.

Chapter 12: Food and Drink

Croatian food is unique and varied because it combines two different cooking styles: the Mediterranean style, which is based on fish, and the Central European style, which is based on filling schnitzel and strudel.

Each part of Croatia also has its own specialties.

Croatia traditional foods

Meat Dishes

A grilled or pan-fried kotlet (chop) or odrezak (fillet or escalope) is usually the main meat dish.

You can cook these in a number of different ways. For example, a kotlet or odrezak cooked nažaru is just a simple grill, a bečkiodrezak (Wiener schnitzel) is fried in breadcrumbs, a pariškiodrezak (Pariser schnitzel) is fried in batter, and a zagrebačkiodrezak (Zagreb schnitzel) is stuffed with cheese and ham. On every Croatian table, you can find Mješanomeso, which means "mixed grill." It usually has a pork or veal kotlet, a few ćevapi, a pljeskavica, and maybe a spicy kobasica (sausage), and it's served with ajvar, a bright red pepper and aubergine relish.

Most of the time, lamb is cooked on a spit. Cres, Rab, and the areas around Zadar and Split are all good places to raise sheep. Along the sides of the road, you can often see restaurants roasting a whole sheep over an open fire to attract tourists.

In Istria and the Adriatic islands, diced lamb is often cooked by slowly baking it under a peka, which is a metal lid that is set on top of hot flames.

Most of the time, meat is grilled or baked instead of stewed. However, goulash (gulaš) is often used as a sauce for pasta, and čobanac (a spicy red stew) is a staple in the southeast.

The word "grah" comes from the haricot beans that are warmed with paprika. Pieces of sausage or pljeskavica are added to this delicious soup.

Dalmatian pašticada, which is beef cooked in wine and prunes, is a main dish that people often eat. Puricasmlincima, which is turkey with baked pasta slivers, is the most popular dish with chicken. It comes from Zagreb and the Zagorje.

Punjenepaprike (peppers filled with rice and meat) and sarma (cabbage leaves filled with a similar mix) are two other main dishes that are high in meat. In the interior of Dalmatia, arambašica is a type of sarma that has more meat and less rice.

Seafood Dishes

Along the coast, you can eat all sorts of fish. As a starter, you can get salataodhobotnice (octopus salad) or salataodjastoga (lobster meat seasoned with olive oil and herbs), which costs a little more.

On the menu, you can get fish either fried, baked, or boiled. Freshly caught fish is usually cooked by grilling. It is sold by weight, with the best fish starting at about 300Kn per kilo in cheap and mid-range restaurants and going up to 400Kn per kilo or more in high-end places.
The wait staff will either tell you what fish they have in stock or show you a tray of fish from which to pick. For one person, a good-sized fish weighs between a third and half a kilo. However, you can always order a big fish and split it between two people.

Swiss chard, or blitva, is a plant that grows in Dalmatia and looks like spinach. It is always served with fish meals and is paired with boiled potatoes and garlic.

There are a lot of different kinds of fish that can be caught in the Adriatic Sea, but some of the best white fish are kovač (John Dory), list (sole), brancin (sea bass), komarčaorada (gilt-head sea bream), and škrpina (scorpion fish). Fish called oslić (hake) is a little less expensive than the others. It is usually given sliced and pan-fried in batter or breadcrumbs instead of grilled, when it is priced by the portion instead of the weight.
Even less expensive are "oily fish," like anchovies and mackerel, which are in the plavariba group. Girice, a small fish that looks a lot like whitebait and is deep-fried and eaten whole, is another cheap option. Brodet, which can also be spelled brudet, is fish that is cooked in red wine and spices. Lignjenažaru (grilled squid) and crnirižot ("black risotto"; made from squid pieces with the ink still on them) are two cheap and common foods that everyone loves.

Rare foods like crab, oysters, mussels, and lobster will be served at more expensive or specialized restaurants. You have to use your fingers to crack open scampi that come in their whole form. A buzara sauce, which is made of garlic and wine, is often served with them.

Below are some common seafoods you can try.

- Pogočaodsrdele is an anchovy pasty that is famous on Vis island.
- Salata od hobotnice is an octopus salad that is served in different ways all over Dalmatia.
- Crnirižot is squid ink risotto, which is a common fish dish all over the country but especially good in Pula.
- Brodetsapalentom is a rich fish stew with polenta that is popular in Istria.
- Shrimps nabuzaru are whole shrimp cooked in oil, tomato, and red wine.
- Grilled fish is served along the coast of Croatia, with platters of the freshest seabass, sole, and John Dory.

Croatian side dishes and salads

You can usually get a carbohydrate side dish like boiled potatoes, chips, rice, or gnocchi, along with a veggie or salad side dish, when you order a main course in Croatia.

In Istria, fuži is made of pasta dough rolled into a cylinder or turned into a twirl. On the island of Krk, šurlice is made of pasta dough, and in Zagreb and the Zagorje, mlinci are lasagne-thin scraps of dough that are boiled and then baked.

On the menu, you can order extra vegetables as separate things. People from Croatia eat a lot of bread, and no matter what else you order, you'll be expected to eat a couple of big slices with your meal.

Zelenasalata (green salad) and mješanasalata (mixed salad) are the most popular types of salad. People also like gherkins (called krastavci) and pickled peppers (called paprike).

Croatian restaurants dessertsand sweets

Desserts that you might find in a restaurant include sladoled (ice cream), torta (cake), and palačinke (pancakes), which are normally served with marmalade, chocolate sauce, or walnuts. In Dubrovnik, you should try rožata, which is like crème caramel but made in the area. You can get ice cream, cakes, and sweets at a slastičarnica. They even have baklava, which is a syrup-covered pastry from the Balkans and the Middle East.

Regional dishes
Food in Istria

The food in Istria is a lot like the food in its nearby countries. In particular, the Italian impact can be seen in the region's specialties, such as pasta, truffles, olive oil, cured ham, and wild asparagus.

The fish from the coast and the hearty meat-based food of Central Europe meet on the Istrian peninsula, making it a true culinary paradise.

No matter if you're looking for a high-class restaurant or a casual inn in the town, the food is always of the highest quality. Oysters (oštrige) from the Limskikanal, cured ham (pršut), wild asparagus (šparoga), and truffles (tartufi) from the hills inland are all delicious foods that are unique to the area. On the kamin, or open fire, Istrian meats like ombolo (smoked pork loin) and kobasice (succulent, fatty sausages) are often cooked.

A lot of people in the area eat fuži (pasta twists) and njoki (gnocchi), which are often made by hand in the more traditional country inns. Istrian olive oil, like olive oil from other parts of Croatia, is mostly made by small farmers or regional cooperatives. This makes sure that the quality is good and that each variety has its own unique flavor.

Malvazija, a crisp white wine made all over the peninsula of Istria, is the most famous wine from the area. Mass-market names like De Mar are fine, but Radovan Family Winery and Clai Craft Winemaker offer better quality.

Teran is a unique local red wine that is a little acidic but very drinkable. Biska, the aphrodisiac mistletoe brandy from the area around Buzet and Hum, is a typical Istrian drink. If you go to Istria, you should try supa at least once. It's a ceramic jug of red wine mixed with sugar, olive oil, and pepper, and it's served with a piece of toast to dip it in.

Truffles: The Istria's culinary gold

In Europe, the woods around Motovun and Buzet are one of the best places to hunt truffles (tartuf). Truffles are underground fungi with a delicate flavor that is a mix of nutty, mushroomy, and sweaty sock. Foodies love them. Since truffles, which look like small tubers, tend to overpower other ingredients, they are only used in small amounts in cooking, like when they are grated over a freshly cooked food or added to a sauce to make it stand out.

Black truffles come into season a little later in the winter and have a slightly less strong flavor. White truffles, which are picked in the fall, are traditionally thought to have the strongest flavor and are normally eaten raw.

The truffle hunting season starts in late September and goes through the fall. Locals and their highly trained dogs go out into the fog of Istria to look for the mushroom.
Most places in the area will have at least one truffle-based dish on the menu at this time, even if it's just a simple truffle-and-pasta dish or an omelette.

From the middle of September to early November, Truffle Days (DaniTartufa) are held in different places in the Motovun/Buzet region. These days may include truffle tastings, live music, or just a lot of drinking in a good mood.

Most people know about the BuzetskaSubotina ("Buzet Saturday") celebration, where a huge truffle omelette is fried in the main street and then eaten by a huge crowd of hungry people.

Food in Dalmatia

Along the coast of Dalmatia, food is very Mediterranean, and fish and seafood are big parts of the menu. It's no surprise that the restaurants on Vis and the nearby islands serve some of the freshest lobster and fish in Dalmatia. The seas off of Vis are home to one of the best fisheries in the Adriatic.

Foods in Zagreb

The food in Zagreb is influenced by the food of its neighbors in Central Europe. The dishes are generally heavier and have meat, potatoes, and root vegetables in them.

Foods in Slavonia

People in Slavonia love hearty stews and meat (usually pork) meals that are cooked in big pots. In Slavonia, paprika is the most popular spice. Smoked meats and pickled veggies are also common, which shows how Austro-Hungarian food has affected the area's food.

Food and drinks in Kvarner Gulf

The Kvarner Gulf has some of the best seafood in all of Croatia. However, the Gulf is best known for its scampi, which do very well here because the bottom is sandy. There are several ways to cook Kvarner scampi, but the traditional dish is škampinabuzaru, which is served in a sauce made of garlic and wine. The scampi are always served whole and without their shells on. You should use your fingers to pry them open and suck out the white meat.

Pag cheese is the best thing that comes from the island. It's hard and spicy, and it's best eaten as a beginning that you can nibble on and enjoy.
On the island of Krk and the close mainland, šurlice, which are long, thin tubes of pasta dough, are a traditional food. They are usually eaten with goulash or lamb stew. When people visit Rab, they should try rabska torta, a marzipan-filled dessert sold in local bakeries. VrbničkaŽlahtina, a great white wine from Vrbnik on Krk's east coast, is the most famous wine from the area.

Food and drink in inland Croatia

The main ingredients on most inland Croatian meals are pork, turkey, duck, and freshwater fish, all of which are known to make you gain weight.

A traditional food in Zagorje and the northeast is roast turkey served with mlinci, which are sheets of pasta that have been torn into odd shapes and topped with tasty turkey juices.

The main thing that defines Slavonia and the Baranja is paprika. Meat and fish are cooked in large pots with lots of the red spice.

Carp, catfish, and pike-perch from the Sava and Drava rivers are often used to make fiš paprika, which is a spicy soup that is served at most restaurants in the southeast and around Osijek. Fišperkelt is a slightly smaller version of the same thing that is often served with noodles that look like tagliatelle.

čobanac, a goulash-like stew with lots of paprika that is served in huge tureens, is what meat eaters eat instead of fiš. Many Slavonian families have one or two pigs, which are usually killed at the end of November as part of the kolinje, or pig cull, that happens every year. As a snack or starter, kulen, a rich sausage flavored with paprika, is the main pork-based treat.

More and more people are interested in the wines of inland Croatia. The family-run farms in Zmajevac and Ilok sell great Graševina (Welschriesling) and Traminac (Gewurztraminer).

Pršut

Pršut is Croatia's most famous starter dish. It's thin pieces of home-cured ham that melt in your mouth. Inland Istria and Dalmatia are where most pršut is made, where families usually have a few pigs. In late fall, the unlucky pigs are killed, and the back legs that are used to make prjut are washed, pickled, and pressed flat under rocks. Then, they are hung outside the house to dry in the bura, which is a cold, dry wind that comes from the middle of Croatia and blows along the coast.

The ham is then hung inside to age until it's ready to be eaten the following summer. During the maturation process, pršut from Dalmatia is often smoked, while that from Istria is left alone. This makes a big difference in the flavors of the two areas' products.

Meals in Croatia

Instead of dinner, lunch (ručak) is the most important meal for Croatians. However, restaurants are used to seeing tourists who eat less at lunch and more in the evening, so they serve a wide range of foods all day long.

Breakfast in Croatia

Unless you're staying in a private room, an apartment, or a campground, food is almost always part of the price of your stay.

Bread rolls, cheese and/or salami pieces, butter and jam are the most basic things that will be in it. Hotels in the middle and upper price range will have a breakfast spread with cereals, scrambled eggs, bacon, and more.

Some Croatian restaurants in tourist areas are starting to serve breakfast. Other than that, not many Croatian cafés or restaurants care to serve breakfast. However, they usually don't mind if you bring bread buns or pastries from a nearby bakery and eat them with your coffee.

Lunch in Croatia

Many Croats eat lunch late in the day, so between 10:30 am and noon, places often serve brunch snacks, which are called marende on the coast and gableci inland.

Most of the time, these are the same as main meat and fish dishes, but they come in smaller amounts and are a great cheap lunch option. Rather than writing things on a menu, people often write them on a board outside.

Snacks In Croatia

Pastries like burek (with ground meat or cheese), zeljanica (with spinach), and krumpiruša (with potato) are sold in most bakeries and slastičarnice. These are classic Croatian foods.

For a heartier snack, try grilled meats from southeast Europe, like ćevapi (rissoles filled with ground beef, pork, or lamb), ražnjići (shish kebab), or pljeskavica (a piece of ground meat that looks like a hamburger). They are all usually served in a lepinja, which is a flat bread bun.

Cooking your own food in Croatia

A supermarket (samoposluga) or an open-air market (tržnica) are good places to get basic foods for cooking at home or for a picnic, like cheese, veggies, and fruit. Most markets open early (around 6 a.m.) and close in the early afternoon. In places with a lot of tourists, they may stay open until late at night. You can get bread at either a grocery store or a restaurant (pekara).

Small stores might only sell a plain white loaf, but most will have a lot of different kinds of bread, from French sticks (francuskibaton or francuz) to wholemeal loaves (punozrnatikruh) and corn bread (kukuruznikruh). But you'll have to point to find what you want because the names of the loaves are different everywhere. Most of the time, a pekara will sell sandwiches with ham, cheese, or pršut inside.

Eating out in Croatia

Most people eat their main meals in a restoran (restaurant) or a konoba (tavern). The latter tends to have more rustic decor but serves mostly the same kinds of food. Another name for a restoran is "gostiona," which means "inn."

If you're going out to eat in Croatia, you should start your meal with pršut, which is Croatia's delicious home-cured ham. It's often served on a plate with cheese. The most famous cheese is paškisir from the island of Pag; it's hard and sour, tasting like a mix of Parmesan and aged cheddar. Cream cheese, on the other hand, is a milder option.

Another delicious food from the area is kulen, a hot sausage from Slavonia that is mixed with paprika. Unless you choose krem-juha, which is a thicker soup, most soups (juha) are clear and light and come with thin noodles.

Trukli is a rich pastry and cheese dish from Zagreb and the Zagorje hills to the north. It is a starter that is hearty enough to be a main meal. Trukli comes in two types: kuhani (boiled) and pečeni (baked). Kuhani štrukli are big balls of dough filled with cottage cheese, while pečeništrukli are made by baking the dough and cheese in a clay dish, making a dish that looks like a mix between a cheese souffle and lasagne.

Croatian street food

In Croatia, street food isn't really a big deal. Pizza is most likely the easiest thing to find when it comes to fast food in Croatia.

But burek cakes made in Croatia are the most common type of street food in that country. Usually filled with meat or cheese, but sometimes you can find sweeter forms that are more like strudel. You can get one of these at a market stall kiosk, a small bakery, or a café.

Vegetarian In Croatian

Croatia has never been known for its vegetarian food, but if you look hard enough, you can usually find something to suit your tastes.

But strict vegans should be careful: many dishes that look like they would be good for them (like risottos and bean soups) are always made with fish or meat stock.

A lot of the time, dishes that are sold as "vegetarian" have ham or chicken in them, even in restaurants that mean well. Grilled veggies that look good may have been cooked on the same grill as the meat dishes, so make sure you ask.

The meat-free starters and side items, on the other hand, can make a nice meal for vegetarians. It's not hard to find pastas with different sauces, mushroom dishes, and big salads. It's pretty common to eat mushroom omelettes (omletsagljiivama) and cheese fried in breadcrumbs (pohanisir). The best bet might be pizzerias and spaghetterias with Italian influences. Most pizzerias serve a pizza vegeterijanska with a variety of seasonal veggies, and most spaghetterias have a variety of meatless pasta dishes, including, if you're lucky, a vegetarian lasagne.

The cheesy štrukli is a traditional food that doesn't have any meat in it, but you won't find it very often on the coast.

The phrase "Ja samvegeterijanac" (vegeterijanka is the feminine form of the word) means "I don't eat meat." Say "Imate li nešto bez mesa" to ask, "Do you have anything that doesn't have meat in it?"

Drinking in Croatia

People drink in a kavana (café), which is usually a big, comfortable space with lots of outdoor sitting that serves all kinds of drinks, including alcoholic and nonalcoholic ones, as well as pastries and ice creams, or in a kafić (café-bar), which is pretty much the same thing but smaller.

Café-bars that try to look like British or, more often, Irish places often use the word "pub." Cafés and café-bars open very early (sometimes as early as 6am) to serve the first espresso to people taking the early-morning boat. However, alcohol isn't served until 9am.

Most places close between 11 p.m. and midnight, but rules are less strict in the summer, when vacation areas' café-bars may stay open until 2 a.m. Aside from the occasional sandwich, not many types of cafés in Croatia serve real food.

Alchohol in Croatia

Beer from Croatia
Light lagers make up most of the beer in Croatia. Mass-market beers like Karlovačko and Ožujsko aren't very interesting, so it's better to try something from a small brewery, like Velebitsko pivo from Gospić or Vukovarsko from Vukovar.

More and more people outside of Zagreb are drinking red beers and porters made by the Medvedgrad brewery. There is also a growing trend for craft beers in Croatia. The Istrian brewery San Servolo makes a wide range of light, red, and dark beers that keep fermenting in the bottle and are sold all over the country.

At the same time, craft brewers in Zagreb like Zmajskapivovara (Dragon Brewery), Nova runda (Another Round), and Varionica (The Brew House) are making new pale ales and porters that you should try if you can find one of the few but growing number of bars that sell them.

When you drink beer from a tap or a bottle, a malopivo (small beer) is 30cl and a velikopivo (large beer) is a half-liter.

Wine from Croatia

In the past few years, Croatia's wine industry has grown by leaps and bounds, thanks in large part to small wineries and family businesses.

There are a lot of good Chardonnays, Cabernets, and Merlots in Croatia, but the native or nearly native grape types are what are really getting people excited.

They are known for their dry white Malvazija and their tannin-rich reds Teran and Refošk. In Dalmatia, you can find better red wines. In the Primošten-Šibenik area, Babić reigns supreme, while Plavacmali, a distant cousin of Zinfandel, rules the south Dalmatian islands and the Pelješac peninsula. The most expensive Plavac wines come from the Dingač and Postup farms on Pelješac. They are some of the best reds in Croatia.

The light whites Pošip and Rukatac are great on the island of Korčula. The medium-dry VrbničkaŽlahtina is famous on Krk, and the flowery white Vugava is famous on Vis.

With Plavacmali, Pošip, and the native white Bogdanjuša, Hvar has so many great things to offer. A lot of eastern Croatia is made up of white Graševina (Welschriesling) and Traminac (Gewurztraminer). The best wines are usually made in the cellars of Kutjevo and Ilok.

Stolinovino, kvalitetnovino, and vrhunskovino are the different types of wine that you can buy in stores and groceries. Everything in the stolno category is cheap and drinkable, but most of the time, the kvalitetno category has better quality at a very fair price. Everything in the Vrhunsko band is really unique.

Bevanda, which is white or red wine mixed with plain water, gemišt, which is white wine mixed with fizzy mineral water, and bambus, which is red wine mixed with cola, are all famous wine-based drinks that are all served cold.

Spirits

Most local spirits, or žestokapića, are grouped together under the word "rakija," which means "brandy." This word also refers to all the native fruit-based firewaters.

If a rakija is made from grapes, it is called loza or lozovača. If it is flavored with something else, it is called travarica (herb brandy), medica (honey brandy), rogačica (carob brandy), orahovača (walnut brandy). Plum brandy (šljivovica) and pear brandy (vilijamovka) are two other types of rakija that are made from different fruits.

You should also try pelinkovac, a juniper-based spirit like Jägermeister, borovnica, a blueberry liqueur, maraskino, a cherry liqueur from Zadar, and biska, an Istrian spirit with a mistletoe flavor. You can find foreign brandies and whiskies just about anywhere.

Soft Drinks, Tea, Coffee In Croatia

Aside from the huge urns of over-stewed brown liquid that motels serve at breakfast, most coffee is very good.
Unless stated otherwise, it is served as a strong black espresso. Kava samlijekom, also known as makijato, has a drop of milk in it, while kava sašlagom has cream in it. Bijela kava, also known as white coffee, tastes like a good latte. Cappuccino is also pretty common.

Most of the time, herbal tea is served. If you want a British-style drink, ask for crničaj (black tea) or indijskičaj (Indian tea). If it says "with a slice of lemon," it means "with milk."

Most of the time, tap water (običnavoda) is free and comes out of the machine when you make an espresso. Mineral water and other soft drinks are often given out in groups of 10cl or dec, which is pronounced "dets." Ask for dvadeca if you want 20cl of mineral water and tri deca if you want 30. Keep in mind that the word đus, which means "juice," generally means orange juice if you want fruit juice.

Chapter 12: Shopping In Croatia

Because it is right next to the world's fashion city, Croatia is a great place for tourists to go shopping. Shopping in Croatia is very different from shopping anywhere else.

You can find big European, local, and high-end brands in malls and small shops. You can also see a different side of shopping in Croatia when you go to the local markets and buy unique Croatian goods.

Five best places to shop in Croatia

Everywhere in this beautiful country, from big cities like Zagreb and Dubrovnik to small towns and villages, shopping is a great time.

1. Arena Centar

Arena Centar is one of the first places you should go shopping in Zagreb, Croatia. People who love shopping will love this place. The shopping center has a lot of great stores, and if you're lucky, you might be able to catch one of the great sales that happen all the time.

This is the biggest indoor shopping mall in the capital city and the surrounding area. It has both high-end brands and chain stores, as well as stores with lower prices. This is the best place to go shopping in Zagreb, but you can also stop by City Center One West if you're in the mood.

2. Mall of Split

Split is one of the best places to shop when you visit Croatia. You will have a great time shopping in Croatia Split.

The city is a great place to shop for clothes, gifts, and fresh food. The Mall of Split is the best place to shop in the city. Designer brands from around the world and Croatia can be found here, along with shops that sell cool clothes made in Croatia.

In the food area, you can take a break and drink a coffee. You should also check out some of the city's well-known spots, such as Croatia, Judita, and Art Studio Naranca.

3. The Portanova

If you are in Osijek, you have to go to this shopping mall. There are shops with big names like H&M, ZARA, New Yorker, and many more in this classic shopping center. You can choose from more than 100 brand names. It is one of the newest and most exciting places to shop in the city. You can take a break from shopping at one of the entertainment centers, which have restaurants, cafés, a bowling place, and a multiplex movie theater.

Portanova is one of the best places to shop in Croatia because it has something for every taste and income level.

4. Shopping Center SRD

There are many shopping stores in Dubrovnik, so if you want to go outlet shopping in Croatia during your trip, you won't be for choice.

Shopping Center Srd is one of the most popular malls in the city. It has a lot of stores that sell both foreign and Croatian brand names.

Shopping in Croatia's Dubrovnik is a lot of fun at stores like Shopping Center Srd, AtlantCentar, and H18 Megastore. Take the time to look around the city for gift and specialty shops. Some great ones are Art Atelier Little House, Uje, Candle Kingdom Dubrovnik Heritage, and many more.

5. SubCity Dubrovnik

You should go to SubCity Dubrovnik if you are in Srebreno and want to shop. It's one of the newest malls in the city, and it's full of stores that sell everything from high-end names to cheap ones, as well as cosmetics and many other things.

It's one of the best places in Croatia to buy clothes. SubCity Dubrovnik also has places to relax like restaurants, cafés, and more where you can watch people go and come.

The mall is close to the beach, which makes it a great spot to spend some money after a day of having fun in the sun. Skatulica, House of Nature, Tedi, and Kokula Art & Craft Shop are some other great places to shop in Srebreno.

Things to Buy When You Go Shopping in Croatia

In Croatia, there is a very large network of shopping malls. Aside from shopping malls, every place in the country has a huge number of gift and specialty shops. You can buy great things to give as gifts or keep as memories in these little shops. Also, there are neighborhood markets where you can get cool things for really low prices.

If you're looking for things to bring back from Croatia, you should check out the local distillates. These are great places to buy gifts for the guys back home, like Lozovac and Slivovitz, which is the local brandy.

Be sure to get Maraschino for women. It's a beautiful cherry liquor with a lovely scent.

For more unique foods from the area, you should visit the island of Pag, which is famous for its Paz cheese.

You can also go to Rijeka, which is known for the gold store Morcic. Some beautiful jewelry made in the traditional Croatian style is for sale.

When you go shopping in Croatia, don't forget to buy some beautiful lace items made by the women there. Each item is different because it has a different, detailed pattern that shows off the skill and time that went into making it.

There are places in Croatia that sell both high-end goods and handmade goods from the area. This means that the country is very different and has something for everyone's taste and budget. There will never be a dull moment on your next trip to Europe. Each city has its own charm and special places to shop that you will never forget.

Chapter 13: Nightlife and Entertainment

Top 15 Places to Have a Good Time at Night in Croatia

1. Deep Makarska

During the day, the pretty port town of Makarska on the coast of Dalmatia has beautiful beaches and a riverfront walkway. At night, it really takes the phrase "party all night" to a whole new level. One of the best bars in Croatia is this secret party spot in a natural cave with a view of the water.

The place, which is often called the "Rave Cave" and is packed with people dancing to the newest beats, has to be seen to be believed. The cave bar has great drinks, great music, and the best views in the area. This is where you can enjoy the best music in Croatia. It has recently risen to the top of the list.

Address:Šetalištefra Jure Radića 5a, 21300, Makarska, Croatia
Hours of service: 9AM-5AM

2. Pag Island's Noa Beach Club

Zrce Beach is known all over the world as one of the hottest beaches in Croatia and for having the best clubs and other fun things to do all day. During the hot summer months, the beach is the place to be for music festivals like Croatia Rocks and Electro Beach. The Noa Beach Club is where all the excitement is. This amazing club, which is right on the water, changes the nighttime in Croatia in a way that no other place does. There are 11 bars with great drinks, loud music, chairs, and the sparkling sea below. This is a great place to get a lot for your money. This is the best place to party in Croatia because there is so much fun to be had.

Address: Zrce Beach, Novalja, Island of Pag 53291, Croatia
Hours of service: 10AM-6AM

3. Boogaloo, Zagreb

This cool spot with a funny name is where most people who want to find the best music in Zagreb, Croatia go. Boogaloo used to be a movie theater but is now a big club with live music performances by some of the best local bands. The music ranges from hard rock to punk to techno. This is a great place to go out at night in Croatia because there are theme nights, foreign gigs, and DJ shows with packed houses. The music is great, and the drinks are even better.

Address: Ul. gradaVukovara 68, 10000, Zagreb, Croatia

4. The Aquarius, Zagreb

There isn't anything else like this two-story club house along Jarun Lake. On the weekends, it can hold up to 2,000 people, making it much better than the competition. This is where you can hear the wide and interesting variety of music that keeps Croatian towns' nightlife alive and well. There are rock and world music acts from around the world as well as DJ sets by international stars that light up the stage. Aquarius has it all. For those who want it all, this is the place to go. It has Goa trance, R&B, House, Electro, and the best acid jazz nights (Kontrapunkt) on Sundays. Yes, those are the best places to party in Croatia!

Address: b. b., Aleja MatijeLjubeka, 10000, Zagreb, Croatia
Hours: 9AM-11PM (Monday-Thursday); 9AM-6AM (Friday-Saturday); Sunday closed

5. Alcatraz, Zagreb

There are three floors of this cozy bar, and each one has a different vibe and sound. This is the best place to go out at night in Croatia. The decor is cool, the staff is friendly, the crowd is young, and the drinks aren't too expensive. Fans of punk rock and old school music should go to the basement. The ground floor plays bar music, and the first floor is where hip-hop and R&B music can be heard. All of the weird art and signs that are stuck on the walls make it feel young and lively. You never know how much fun you'll have here, so having fun here could be one of the best things to do in Croatia.

Address: Preradovićevaul. 12, 10000, Zagreb, Croatia
Hours: 7am-4am (mon-sat), 9am-12am (Sunday)

6. Banje Beach Restaurant and Nightclub in Dubrovnik.

If you go to this great club in the afternoon, it suddenly changes into a super-cool nightclub by the evening, where you might run into some famous people who are out partying. The terrace on the roof, which faces the beach in Dubrovnik, is the best spot for great views and drinks. A lot of people know the amazing nightclub for its hot parties. DJs set the floor on fire, and before you know it, the night is over. You can't miss this part of Dubrovnik, Croatia's nightlife.

Address: Ul. Frana Supila 10A, 20000, Dubrovnik, Croatia
Hours: Daily, 10am-5am

7. The Kiva Bar

The party crowds at this cozy rock bar are here most days of the week. It's a great place to experience Croatian nightlife because everyone dances like no one is watching. Kiva Bar has the best nightlife in Croatia because of its happy vibes, great music, and nice people. Kiva is tucked away in an alleyway behind the quay and is probably the most famous cult bar on the island. It has great drinks and a wide range of music (rock n roll, jazz, funk, and more!) that makes everyone want to dance every night.

Address: Fabrika 26, 21450, Hvar, Croatia
Hours: 9PM-2:30AM (Summer); 9am-2:30am (Winter, Monday-Friday)

8. Carpe Diem

A ferry from the mainland takes you this awesome club with an enviable view of the harbor with fantastic outdoor seating. When it gets dark, house music, party vibes, and drinks take you to a happy place where you can rock to the beats. You can enjoy great drinks and take in the view of the harbor, or you can join the fun at the Carpe Diem beach party. Carpe Diem is one of the best places to go out at night in Hvar, Croatia. It's the coolest bar in town and the busiest club at night, and famous people often go there.

Address: Riva 32, 21450, Hvar, Croatia
Hours: Daily, 9am-2am

9. Hula HulaBar and beach

What more could you want than the grooviest music, the wildest people, and the most beautiful sunsets? There are great drinks at Hula Hula, a fun beach bar where you can start dancing to great music early in the evening. Croatia's nightlife comes to life at this cool spot, where people party crazy at sunset on the beach with cool DJs.

Address: Vlade Avelinija 10, Hvar, Croatia
Hours: Daily, 8am-11pm

10. Akvinta Party Boat, Makarska

If you're tired of the nightlife in the heart of Croatia, take the Akvinta Party Boat to the beautiful Makarska Riviera for the best nightlife in the country. There is a lot going on at night in Makarska, even though it is a quiet town during the day. Get cheap beer, warm weather, and great music to make your nights seem like they're from another world. As you sail off into the sunset on your honeymoon in Croatia, start the party.

11. The Academia Club Ghetto in Split

For nightlife, Split is the best place to stay in Croatia. You can find secret bars and enjoy a lively atmosphere there. If you're only in Split for the night, go to Academia Club Ghetto right away for a fun time. People say it is one of the best clubs in Croatia, and it is inside Diocletian's Palace. Travelers love to crash at this little secret gem in the evening. In Split, one of the best things to do is go to a party here.

Address: 10 Dosudulica, 21000 Split, Croatia

12. The Club Crkva in Rijeka

In Rijeka, Crkva is one of the best places to party in Croatia. It is right next to the Rijeka River. If you believe what party animals say, it is one of the coolest and most beautiful places to have a party. In Croatia, this club is where you should go for the brightest nightlife. The coolest DJs play there. Drink and be around things that will make you feel drunk.
Address: Ružićevaul. 22, 51000 Rijeka, Croatia

13. The Club Aurora and Primosten

If you want to have a great time, Club Aurora should be on your list of the best places to party in Croatia. This club has been around longer than most in Croatia and has been a part of many dance and music trends. There are six bars, three dance floors, a chill-out lounge area, and an open-air area with palm trees. Are you still not sure that this is the best place?

Address : Kamenar b.b., 22202 Primošten, Croatia

14. The Aquarius Club in Zagreb

If you're looking for a good list of bars in Croatia, you can't miss this one. This is one of the first clubs in Croatia where famous DJs got their start. It opened in 1992. Right next to Lake Jarun, this is the perfect place to go on the ultimate dancing spree, which you will definitely enjoy.

Address: 19 Aleja MatijeLjubeka, 10000 Zagreb, Croatia

15. Zagreb Art Gallery

The Gallery club in Zagreb is one of the best places to go out at night in Croatia. It's a mix of modern and hip. This club is one of the best places to try real Croatian nightlife. It is close to Jarun Lake. The inside of the club is fancy, and there are great beats playing in the background, making it the perfect place to have the best night possible.

Address: Aleja MatijeLjubeka 10, 10000 Zagreb, Croatia

Croatia's nightlife is just as fun as walking around its charming towns during the day because there are so many places to go and things to do. Croatia also has some of the best and craziest music festivals, such as the Ultra Music Festival in Split every summer.

Chapter 14: In conclusion

I will tell you 10 things you need to know before you go to Croatia in this last part. Here are some of them:

1. Be focused
2. Do not just visit Dubrovnik.
3. Get the best beds by booking early.
4. Enjoy the island life
5. Take a wild walk
6. Learn their culture
7. Eat well
8. Drink responsibly
9. Learn some slang
10. Your health matters

1. Be focused

Because Croatia has so much to offer, it can be hard not to try to fit too much into your first trip. But you should really fight the urge—if you only have a short amount of time, focusing on just one or two places will be more useful.

For instance, if you only have a week, you could split your time between the coast and Zagreb, which is known as Croatia's center of cool for many reasons. You should only stay in the city for a couple of nights. That will give you time to enjoy the beautiful Adriatic.

For longer trips, it's worth going further away to see beautiful places like the Plitvice Lakes and the castles of Zagorje.

2. Do not just visit Dubrovnik.

Yes, Dubrovnik is worthy of Lord Byron's "Pearl of the Adriatic" title.
But why not think about going to Split instead? A beautiful UNESCO Heritage Site is in the middle of Croatia's second-largest city. Specifically, the amazing Roman Palace of Diocletian. Split is also a great place to eat, drink, shop, and have fun in general.

You might also want to look into why you should go to Zadar and Pula on your next trip to Croatia. Pula has a huge Roman amphitheater that is on the UNESCO list and some of the best restaurants in Istria.

3. Get the best beds by booking early

It may seem obvious, but if you want to find the best place to stay in Croatia, you should really do your homework and book early.

There are many places to stay in Dubrovnik, but it's popular all year (see above), so book early if you want to stay somewhere with an Old Town feel, like the stylish Villa Dubrovnik.

Want to look good in Spilt? You'll need to act quickly if you want to get a private room in the Diocletian's Palace. You should do the same thing if you want to visit any of Croatia's most famous islands in the summer.

Hvar is a popular place for couples, party animals, and families, which is a wide range of people, so hotels fill up quickly. Same thing happens when you try to book a place to stay on Mljet, an island paradise for nature fans and lovers of love.

4. Enjoy the island life

There is an island in Croatia for everyone, from people who like to party all the time to people who just want to relax without a car. To be more precise, Croatia has islands for all of us.

You should visit more than one island if you have time. There are many safe and cheap ferry services, so you could easily go to a few during a trip of a reasonable length.
On the other hand, the Adriatic Sea is a great place for sailing vacations, which is why Croatia is one of the most famous sailing spots in Europe.

If you'd rather have someone else steer, check out our totally customizable Dalmatia sailing trip. It takes all the work out of planning and puts you in the hands of professionals.

5. Take a wild walk

Croatia is known for its beaches and sun, but the best way to see its wilder areas is to get active, especially if you like to go on adventures outside. Croatia was even on our list of the best action vacations in the world.

Paklenica National Park is a great place to hike and climb, and Plitvice Lakes National Park is a real paradise with its beautiful mountains, lakes, and waterfalls. The Plitvice Lakes are a UNESCO World Heritage Site and have twelve trails to discover.

North Velebit National Park has even more wild areas that haven't been touched by humans. The Premuzic Trail is a very interesting hike because it goes through rocky cliffs, limestone peaks, wildflower meadows, and pine woods.

6. Learn their culture

In addition to soaking up the sun and loving the great outdoors, Croatia has a lot to offer tourists who want to learn about its history and culture. There are huge ancient monuments as well as moving landmarks from the 20th century.

We've already talked about the Roman sites in Pula and Split. When we go further back in time, Varazdin is a beautiful Baroque town, and Dubrovnik is one of the best-preserved medieval towns in the world.

Want to learn more about current history? In 1991, 2000 citizens defended Vukovar during the 87-day Siege of Vukovar. There are many museums and other places in Vukovar that honor this event.

7. Eat very well

Due to its location, Croatia has the best of both Mediterranean and Central European cuisines. Our guide to eating and drinking in Croatia shows you how to enjoy the best of both worlds.

Meals on your own? Organic food from local stores can be used to make delicious picnics. This is one of the best travel tips for Croatia for foodies and budget travelers alike.

There are many great seafood places in Croatia, and every day, fish from the Adriatic is brought in to fill their menus. The fish, stews, and anchovy pasties on Vis made it our choice for the best Croatian island for foodies.

Like cheese? Go to Pag to try the spicy goat cheese that grows there. On the shore, Istria is the best place to find truffles. In Buzet, you can find out how to join the truffle trail.

8. Drink responsibly

To go with all that great food, you need something really special. And, thank goodness, Croatia has a lot of great drinks.

Croatia's wines are some of the best in the world, but because they are so popular in their own country, it will be hard to find them in stores back home. So enjoy them while you can.

Those who like full-bodied reds should try the Dingac, and those who like dry whites will fall in love with Pošip. Istria is known for Malvasija, which is another dry white wine that goes well with fish. When it comes to dessert wines, Malvasia from the Dubrovnik area is a great choice.

Like food tours, you can take a wine tour no matter where you are in Croatia. If you're on Hvar, for example, this three-hour walk lets you taste four different kinds of wine.

It's not just about the wine, though. If you're ever in Croatia, you should try a shot of rakija, which is a fiery fruit spirit almost always made from grapes.

9. Learn some slang

For those of you who have been enjoying eating and drinking like a local, why not try to speak the language too? Even though a lot of people speak English and it can be hard to speak Croatian, learning even a little will help a lot. Before buying a Croatian Phrasebook and Dictionary, here are some things you should know:

Good morning - Dobro jutro, which you say like this: "doh-broh you-troh"

Good day - Dobar dan, which you say like this: "doh-bahr dahn"

Good evening - Dobra večer, which you say like this: "doh-brahve-cher"

Goodbye - Doviđenja, which you say like this: "doh-vee-jen-yah"

Please - Molim, which you say like this "moh-leem"

Thanks - Hvala, which you say like this "hva-lah"

"Cheers"- Živjeli, which you say like "ji-vo-li"

10. Your health matters

It's always a good idea to get travel insurance, even if you're just going away for the weekend.

Bring a European Health Insurance Card (EHIC) with you if you live in the EU. You can get basic health care from the government in Croatia with this, but it won't cover you for medical care that you need to continue or care that isn't urgent. That's why you need good travel insurance.

In Croatia, you can call 112 for all kinds of emergency services, like police, fire, and ambulances. 194 will connect you to medical help in an emergency. The number for the maritime search and rescue service is 195. If you need help on the road, call 1987.

Have a safe trip, and have a great time in the beautiful city of Croatia.

Made in the USA
Las Vegas, NV
05 April 2025